Jane

ALWAYS EAT THE
HARD CRUST OF
THE BREAD

from Dennis

via Mommie

ALWAYS EAT THE HARD CRUST OF THE BREAD

Recollections and Recipes from
My Centenarian Mother

DAVID MAZZARELLA

iUniverse, Inc.
Bloomington
In association with TPD Publishing LLC

Always Eat the Hard Crust of the Bread
Recollections and Recipes from My Centenarian Mother

iUniverse books may be ordered through booksellers or by contacting:

iUniverse
1663 Liberty Drive
Bloomington, IN 47403
www.iuniverse.com
1-800-Authors (1-800-288-4677)

ISBN: 978-1-4759-1394-1 (sc)
ISBN: 978-1-4759-1395-8 (hc)
ISBN: 978-1-4759-1396-5 (e)

Library of Congress Control Number: 2012906717

Printed in the United States of America

iUniverse rev. date: 6/25/2012

Dedication

For my inspirer and wife Christine, and all those
in whose veins Benigna's blood flows.

Contents

Part I: The Family

Part II: Recipes

Part III: The "Holy Grail"

Introduction

Benigna Preziosi Mazzarella, my mother, wasn't much given to profound sayings. Sometimes she'd parcel one out as a sort of soundbite. Her favorite was probably "Other people are not like us," referring to what she saw as the family's hallmarks—a certain stoicism, a tendency toward accommodation, a slowness to anger. She said it with both pride and resignation. Other people could be selfish, lacking in good manners, but not "us." She might say this after some perceived betrayal or a merchant's sleight of hand.

I kept coming back to that maxim as I contemplated the astonishing amount of time my mother spent on this earth—one hundred and seven years and nine months. I didn't think of the phrase only in the same way she did, in regard to the family; I also thought of it in regard to *her*.

Other people were not like *her*. Other people, at least a lot of them, ate and drank in a way that gave them big bellies and sugary blood. She ate simply all her life; fatty food was an enemy. Other people dreamed fitfully of retirement at sixty-five or earlier. She worked in a factory until she was eighty, and wished she could have gone on for years more. She lived her way, somehow following much of the advice in those self-improvement books she never read, and never would have dreamed of reading.

And yet, as I tried to explore the reasons for her longevity, it occurred to me that her life seemed exceedingly mundane. She was a child of the twentieth century, all of it, having been born in 1900 in southern Italy.

(She died in 2008.) Childhood was spent at the apron of her mother, a strong-willed widow. Barely out of her teens, the pretty Benigna joined the flood of what must have been an anxious emigration to a strange land, the United States. She married a *paisano,* a home townsman, for whom she had had little time in the old country, but with whom she became reacquainted once he had emigrated too. They raised three children, first in the teeming city of Newark, New Jersey, and then in one of that city's all-American suburbs, South Orange. Outwardly, it was a life familiar to millions, of home and hearth, decades of work, a little upward mobility, some friends and relatives, and occasional plain pleasures, followed finally by tranquil old age and death.

Seen this way, her life seemed the epitome of ordinariness, except that it also embodied a perfect combination for longevity: amazing genes, adherence to the famous Mediterranean diet, and almost compulsive physical activity (mostly in the form of walking, fast). The genes were a gift; the Mediterranean diet was adapted to her tastes (Down with garlic! Her eating habits are on display in the cookbook chapters that follow.); and the exercise was a hallmark of her personality.

She imbued her days with an energy all her own, flowing determinedly from one phase of her life to the next, always the center of attraction despite never having lobbied for the honor. Her personality was complex; her enormous empathy made her an ideal confidante. She had an uncanny way of sensing the feelings of others, so it wasn't possible to keep any subsurface troubles from her for long. Neither was it easy for her to keep her own concerns hidden; with lips tight and mouth turned downward, she would signal that something was bothering her. There were times she would let it all out too, even with salty words that momentarily challenged the family's vaunted reputation for stoicism. This pointed to a central contradiction of Mama's. She could be demure and submissive, or forceful and steely. One mood was an overlay of the other, depending on the circumstance.

It was not all smooth sailing. As did millions of families, hers struggled through the Depression, emerging whole and healthy. In midlife and beyond, she had to worry about and care for a few needy relatives, including her funny, slightly eccentric, hypochondriacal husband, who thought of her as a cat because of her looks and movements. For these relatives, all of her generation, she was a nurturer, though at times a reluctant one. For her children, grandchildren, great-grandchildren, and others in an expanding circle, she was a *happy* nurturer. Could that attribute have led to a long life?

As to how Mama saw herself, that was lacking in complication. She just plowed ahead, one day after the other. She seemed to have no regard for her age. It were as if, at ninety-five, she thought of herself as sixty, or fifty, or forty. Only in her last years did she seem to turn more philosophical: "Ah," she would sigh, "we all have to die sometime." But you got the idea she didn't believe that either. Curiously, this attitude was infectious, in the sense that the rest of us also believed she could and would go on forever. Or, at least, we couldn't envision the day she would leave us. Even when she passed the age of one hundred, news that she was sick with something or other was dismissed. She would recover. Invariably, she did. And while nonchalant about her clocking off of the years, we knew we would never match them, and probably wouldn't come close.

What might Mama's life tell us about longevity, aside from the presence of good genes, which many people have but still don't reach her years? Maybe only that moderation has a role. And regularity of habits. And a disciplined palate. And a stiff spine. And pleasure found in work. And laughter. And a carrying of one's years lightly. And love and protection of family—even some of its more nettlesome characters.

In these pages is a buffet of facts, stories, personal foibles, sayings, and recipes that may serve to flesh out those attributes.

Food, Genes, Energy, and Some "Crosses"

Foremost among Mama's special traits was her mastery in the kitchen, though she hardly would have called it that. A cautious eater herself, she had a knack for turning out dish after dish that found favor among family, friends, and even tradesmen, whom she often rewarded with treats as they worked around the house.

There is no single fountain-of-youth discovery in the search for links between Mama's longevity and her eating habits. She didn't know anything about special diets and health-food fads. But there were certain tastes and practices of hers that were healthful by any standard, and, I believe, helped her reach to within three months of her one-hundred-and-eighth birthday before she died of pneumonia on January 20, 2008. And the food she cooked tasted good, very good, to four generations of the family. I describe in this book some dishes that I think a general audience might find original.

Then there were Mama's genes. Her mother died at ninety-five, never having left her village in southern Italy. One of her sisters, Rosaria, who also never left Italy, died at ninety. Another sister, Eleanor, who came to America on the same boat as Mama in 1920, died at ninety-seven. Alas, the men in Mama's Preziosi family did not fare as well. The two brothers of these sisters died young. And their father died when Mama, the youngest in the family, was only five. Did they not get *the* genes? Or was this precious endowment overridden by what reputedly was a certain hard-living style on the part of the men in the family?

The case for the ladies' genes, at least, is made nicely by Eleanor. While my mother and Rosaria were relatively ascetic at the table, Eleanor was a reckless gourmand who still lived into her nineties. While Eleanor was heavy and sedentary, Mama was slim and known for her quickness of step. She walked everywhere, worked many years without complaint, and asked only for minimal help in house-cleaning. She needed that kind of energy to enable her to take care of people, even if they represented *croci* (crosses) for her to bear. These "crosses" were embodied in a few relatives who were contemporaries of hers. Eleanor was one. Others were her husband and his brother-in-law. Mama was central in their lives, just as she was in those of her children, grandchildren, and great-grandchildren.

The three needy relatives made Mama feel irritation, sympathy, or both. In working to satisfy those needs, Mama seemed, paradoxically, to gain strength, or at least a kind of staying power that avoided having the years be a burden to her. When these close relatives were gone, there was no one of that generation in the entire family left on earth, except Mama. They are remembered in three successive chapters in this book.

Wizard of the Kitchen

Genes and lifestyle aside, did Mama's eating habits, especially, give her a decade over her sister Eleanor? They had an effect, no doubt. What distinguished all of her cooking was simplicity, in substance and preparation, although some dishes, like her homemade pasta, required a measure of manual effort.

In Mama's obituary in the *Star-Ledger* of Newark, she was described as a "wizard of the kitchen." This is not to be taken to mean she was a "serious" cook. I never saw her crack open a cookbook or even read a recipe. She hardly talked about food, except to ask what one might want for dinner on a given night. Cooking is just what the lady of the house did, without fanfare, excessive experimentation, or philosophizing.

In Mama's case, it had to be so, because she worked for most of her life. She was a seamstress and retired at eighty. For years before her retirement, the owner of the factory where she worked, Mr. D'Allesandro, had been picking her up at home in the morning, eager to have one of his best employees at the sewing tables. (It was said that in her younger years, she sewed with such speed that her arm was a blur.) She went gladly to work with the boss. Her time in the factory gave some structure to her life, and she could soak up gossip from the other seamstresses amid the smell of sweat, scissored wool, and steam from the pressing machines. She finally quit, she said, only because she didn't want her old friends to get the impression she was "*la vecchia fissata con i soldi*" (an old lady obsessed with money).

For Mama, in her working years, to organize dinner, it took a little shopping on the way home and, *chop, chop*, the construction of a quick but ample meal. The family—my father Pasquale, my older siblings Bud and Alba, and I—gathered to find everything prepared, having taken for granted that dinner would be there, without previous discussion or fuss.

With few exceptions, then, the recipes in this book are relatively uncomplicated. Some need more time, as sometimes Mama cooked a part of the repast early, finishing it off when she returned from work. On weekends—and all the time after her retirement—she spent quiet time looking after the dishes that required more attention. Until her one hundredth year, when she was recovering from a broken hip that prevented her from standing at length in the kitchen, she cooked dinners, even the traditional Italian Christmas Eve Feast of Many Fishes. (She lived in her own house until, at a hundred and seven, she got sick and went to a hospital three months before her death.)

Regardless of the cooking and preparation time needed, there are no gourmet gooey things in this collection of recipes, no fancy fusions. Though innovative in the context of the traditional Italian-American kitchen, many of the dishes would seem stark indeed next to the exotic concoctions found nowadays on cooking shows on television. There were some dishes of Mama's that were delicious but done so plainly that I have not included them among the recipes: broiled turkey for example, or lamb chops, which she just plopped into a toaster-broiler for a few minutes, or rice in chicken broth and butter to soothe a troubled stomach. Some dishes that Mama made in the earlier years, such as calf's brains and tripe, are excluded for reasons that, at least for me, are self-evident.

But there were unusual specialties of Mama's too, such as the smooth, pepper-and-onion-flavored marinara sauce, the celery leaf and prosciutto pasta, the vinegar chicken, and the zucchini parmigiana, that I hope can be considered worth the price of admission. And I will also share a dish so special, so dependent on a single mysterious ingredient, that it may be hard for you to ever taste it. It will only be possible to experience if you are very close to a relatively rare possessor or purveyor of the ingredient here in America, or if you travel all the way to Italy, where the unique specialty is consumed in abundance in only a few small villages tucked close together in the folds of the Apennine mountains.

A word about the compilation of these recipes. For years, I, my sister Alba, and other relatives have routinely made several of the dishes, sticking as closely as possible to Mama's own kitchen maneuvers. I take pride in the tomato sauce, Alba in the parmigiana, and cousin Rosanella Ferrara in the homemade pasta. Various members have tackled the tricky vinegar chicken, some with better results than others. We're all amateurs, and have shamelessly borrowed an idea here and there from real chefs, their contributions duly noted.

A Videotape at Ninety

Additionally, when she was ninety, Mama allowed herself to be videotaped in the kitchen as she made various things—pasta, meat, and fish dishes; raisin cookies; and so forth. The tape was labeled "Grandma Cooks!" She lived for a good many years after, but the family didn't know at the time that she would, and we wanted a record. (Into her seventies, eighties, and early nineties, Mama heard a common refrain on her birthday: *"Per cent'anni!"* meaning "May you live a hundred years!" As she approached a hundred, the wish seemed grossly inappropriate, and when she reached a hundred, it, of course, went out the window altogether.)

Here and there, some liberties have been taken with recipes, adjusting slightly some measurements (including garlic!), for instance, or moderating some cooking times, or including some other recipes alongside Mama's. These should be considered "in the spirit" of Mama's cooking, meaning they are relatively simple and not laden with fat. Mostly, the dishes showcased here are of her own inspiration, lovingly but unpretentiously prepared. Health purists may be surprised by some recipes requiring frying, though the frying was always quick and light.

On the way to the recipes are chapters on Mama the person, and on those last contemporaries of hers, described just as Mama perceived, endured, and fed them.

This volume joins the many accounts of cooking by other mamas and grandmas, which can fill a small library. The phenomenon crosses national boundaries and goes back a long way. More than a quarter-century ago, while I was living in Italy, food purists there began rebelling against the fast, mass-produced foods that were appearing even in that country of tradition-bound cuisine.

Newspapers and magazines competed in the 1970s to give readers the most coveted *ricette della nonna,* or grandmother's recipes. In Rome, a top-flight restaurant specializing in Venetian fare, across Piazza Colonna from the prime minister's office and parliament—and thus frequented by many distinguished, dark-suited Italian gentlemen—had this remarkable sign on the front door: "Mother's Home Cooking," in English.

There is a restaurant in Staten Island, New York, whose owner went to Italy to recruit eight *nonnas* to serve grandmotherly specialties at his establishment. Cookbooks extolling "mother's" or "grandmother's" cooking know no ethnic bounds. You can find accounts of the cooking of matriarchs who are Greek, Polish, Korean, Mexican, German, Chinese, Croatian, Lebanese, Italian, and Jewish. There are grandma's cookbooks from the American South and other U.S. regions. There is a *Great-Grandmother's Cookbook*, first published in 1876 and still available for those, presumably, who favor slow, slow cooking. There are cookbooks of combined heritage, such as a Jewish-Sicilian matriarchal cookbook. And, there is a *Grandma's Marijuana Cookbook*, vetted for legality, presumably.

As matriarchs, mamas and grandmas inspire their descendants to cook with "heart and passion." That's what so much of the literature says. This is the story of a matriarch with heart and passion who remarkably kept cooking up to the age of one hundred, and who never read a word of any of it.

Part I:
The Family

Benigna's Story

M y father used to say that my mother was a cat incarnate. She resembled one, he said, with her smallness, soft cheeks, and enigmatic but expressive dark brown eyes. And she could act like one, clicking far ahead of him with resolute feline steps on walks through stores, or issuing a hiss of strong words if backed into a virtual corner.

She didn't curl up on anybody's lap, but with Papa next to her on the couch, asleep with the television on, she did the next best thing: she slipped her tiny feet into his pants pocket to keep them warm. All that lacked was the purring. This foot-in-pocket trick agitated Papa to no end when he woke up.

But her greatest resemblance to a cat lay in the nine lives, or maybe more, that helped her live to one hundred seven years and nine months. She was part of the fastest-growing segment of the U.S. population: centenarians. Supercentenarians—those a hundred and ten or older—are rarer. At this writing, there were only thirteen such individuals in the United States whose ages were validated, according to the Los Angeles Gerontology Research Group. In Mama's home country of Italy, there were eleven confirmed supercentenarians. Those numbers will grow, as modern medicine finds more ways to keep people alive longer.

Mama didn't need men and women of science to help her reach such an extreme old age, however, and was just a little more than two years shy of supercentenarian status. She made do with good genes, healthful eating and living, and a good measure of feline-like good fortune.

Luck entered into it when some maladies that could have done her in at an earlier age turned out to be surmountable: a growth in her throat during her forties that was found to be noncancerous; angina attacks in her sixties that were cured more effectively with family harmony than with drugs; severe diverticulitis that disappeared by itself in her eighties; and a broken hip at ninety-five that caused hospital staffers to write her off, only to see her bounce back. The staffers could hardly have been blamed for their pessimism. According to the American Academy of Orthopaedic Surgeons, about a quarter of "hip fracture patients *over age fifty* [my emphasis] die within twelve months after injury because of complications related to the injury and the extended recovery period." Mama was nearly twice that age.

Then there were the shingles that caused the crown of her head and the back of her neck to itch and hurt mightily. She was just turning a hundred and three. How sad, we thought, that her final days should be so pain-wracked. But then, surprisingly, the shingles faded and Mama plowed on for four years more.

She had a simple way of dealing with illness: she asked her doctor if whatever she had was fatal. If the doctor said no, she stopped fretting and did as she was told. I was in her hospital room the night before she was to have an operation to repair a faulty tear duct in her left eye. She was in her late eighties. Mama fixed the doctor with a cat-like glare, that wide-pupiled look, conveying a mixture of curiosity and fear.

"Can you die from this?" she asked.

The doctor found this mildly amusing. "No," he said firmly, and Mama went back to watching the news on the hospital television.

Even more than her ability to overcome a variety of ailments, Mama's strict habits relating to food and lifestyle are what enabled her to live to a hundred and seven.

The life of Benigna Preziosi (pronounced BEH-NEEN-YA, a word that means "kind") spanned the entire twentieth century. And from all that we know, she cooked and ate at the end of that century, and the remaining years of her life, more or less as she had at the beginning of it, as a girl in her hometown of Mirabella Eclano, in Italy. By that, I mean she cooked simply and healthfully.

She did not learn to cook from her mother. Her mother ran a sundries shop and couldn't be bothered with kitchen duties. Mama and her sisters Eleanor and Rosaria taught themselves how to cook. And having emigrated, Mama was not much impressed by the bounty of edibles to be found in America as the century wore on. She ate meat, even liked to gnaw on the bones, but not the fatty kinds of meat, and certainly not the gigantic red-meat cuts suburbanites were grilling in backyards. Hamburgers and hot dogs were only for other people (including, occasionally, others of us in the family). And although I ate a TV dinner once in a while, as a novelty, I never saw one in front of Mama, ever.

Fish she ate with no reservation, and all kinds. It was always prepared simply, without extravagant sauces. The exception was Christmas Eve, when the traditional Italian seafood feast required shrimp, lobster, eel, calamari, and flounder to be broiled, fried, or buried in tomato sauce.

She also ate pasta without hesitation. Her favorites were handmade fusilli, orecchietti, gnocchi, cavatelli, ravioli, and pappardelle (full length or in pieces). Of course, she also enjoyed store-bought pasta in dry form—spaghetti, penne, shells, and rigatoni. Some of her pasta dishes were unusual, but they were always delicious. As mentioned, many of her recipes follow later on.

Garlic, Raw Tomatoes, Oregano, Fat, Wine—Ugh

For a native of Italy, Mama had some eating idiosyncrasies.

She was not fond of garlic, eating it only in certain dishes and in certain forms. In some sauces, she'd drop in a clove and extract it before it wilted.

She didn't eat raw tomatoes with the skin on and seeds inside, except, rarely, in a Caprese salad with mozzarella. Her basic tomato sauce had to be made with purée, not cut tomatoes. I wondered if there were some below-the-surface antitomato sentiment in her part of Italy, from the time when the fruit Columbus brought to Europe from the New World was regarded as poison.

Mama also had little use for another Italian kitchen standby, oregano. She used it sparingly and almost exclusively on the above-mentioned Caprese. She might drop a pinch on roasted peppers, or on pasta with fagioli (beans).

Though she occasionally ate meat, she had an aversion to fat. She would stand over a pot of soup or meat gravy as long as it took to spoon out all the fat that rose to the top. It was simply a matter of taste, not any thought of gaining a health advantage. (I inherited the disdain for fat, or it was trained into me. To this day, I slice most of the fat from any kind of meat before eating it. I know, "the flavor's in the fat." For me, however, the fat *kills* the flavor, which was Mama's position as well. Sorry.)

Another unusual trait for an Italian person: Mama drank not a glass of wine, or any alcoholic beverage, her entire life. To entertain guests, Papa would sometimes force her to swallow a small amount of wine, and then laugh as her eyes rolled dizzily. She had a word or two for Papa under her breath in such circumstances. Her disdain for alcohol was not necessarily because she thought it would do her harm; she just didn't like it.

Lest you think Mama would eat only her own familiar Italian dishes, consider that she really liked two distinctly non-Italian types of cuisine: Chinese and Indian. She could tolerate only a touch of hot pepper in her own cooking, but had no problem with some edgy shrimp stir-fry or vegetable samosas. There was something appealing for her about these two Asian cuisines, which were so different from her own cooking, but, like hers, lean, delicious, and true to an ethnic standard.

Mama liked plenty of healthful foods, including vegetables (especially spinach, green beans, baked beans, and broccoli rabe), fruits (especially grapes, bananas, figs, and baked apples), and nuts. She especially liked walnuts, whose shells she cracked with her teeth. A researcher at the University of Scranton says he has found that walnuts are the "best" nuts, at least in one respect: they are more abundant in antioxidants than any other—one example of Mama mysteriously knowing things about food that science could corroborate. She made potatoes in all forms, except as french fries.

More of note than what she ate was how she ate. She ate with restraint and orderliness. This was true in her self-sufficient years, whether working or not working, as well as several years into her second century, when she had a daily companion or, on weekends, my sister Alba cooking for her.

Breakfast for Mama was a sort of formal affair. She took it seated, with real dishes, cups, and glasses, rather than with paper and plastic substitutes, as people in a hurry might do. The meal consisted of a single cup of coffee with milk and sugar, a single but large piece of crusty bread with butter, a multivitamin, and an egg. Mama's relationship with eggs was evolutionary. In the early years, she would consume them raw, punching holes in both ends and sucking out the insides. Later, she ate eggs hard-boiled, or rather she ate the whites and gave the yolks to little birds in the backyard. Later still, the standard morning practice was to have the egg, yolk and all, medium-boiled. Such was Mama's standard breakfast, year after year.

Only the Hard Crust, Please

As for bread, Mama had a certain way of eating that too. First of all, she didn't eat much of it. And she didn't eat the soft white insides, except rarely, when the bread was toasted. It was the hard crust of Italian loaves that she loved to chew on, and that she recommended to all.

"Always eat the hard crust of the bread," she'd say, "the insides sit on your stomach." The East Orange Bakery, located in the town of the same name in New Jersey, dispatched bread to Mama long after it had stopped delivering to other customers. Two crusty loaves, one oblong, the other round, would land on Mama's screened-in front porch, in neighboring South Orange, every Saturday morning.

At least one other centenarian had the same idea about bread. In the late seventies, I was editor of a newspaper in central New Jersey. One day, the city editor sent a reporter to write a story about a local woman, of Italian ancestry, who had just turned one hundred. When the reporter returned, she said she had asked the woman the obligatory question: how do you live so long? To which the woman told the reporter that, when eating bread, one ought to eat only the crust. Puzzled, the reporter wondered whether the woman meant this metaphorically. No, I told the reporter, the woman was just in unknowing agreement with my mother's mantra.

As I was writing this account of Mama's habits, I came across a recommendation from *Prevention* magazine headlined "Ask for the Heel." It said, "Bread crust has up to eight times more pronyl-lysine—an antioxidant that fights cancer—than what's in the center." I smiled, imagining what Mama would have said about those big words confirming what her own instincts had told her.

Mama provided other food-related nuggets of information. Whether she came upon them herself or was parroting what she had heard from the doctors to whom she rushed us children at the first sign of a fever, I don't know. A couple of examples: "Never eat bananas and drink water at the same time" (evidently to avoid indigestion) and "Eating nuts is as good as eating meat" (not exactly true, but close).

Onto the rest of Mama's daily fare:

Lunch, whether she was working or, later, in her retired years, usually was a sandwich or soup and some fruit. A cup of tea or coffee with milk and a biscuit or two comprised a late-afternoon interlude, the only between-meals food she would eat. Quite often in her later years, there was company for these leisurely snacks, lady friends who came to bring Mama the latest gossip and to fuss over her. She held court, laughing easily but usually content to listen rather than contribute much to the tales being told.

Mama was not one to drink the recommended quart or more of water daily. A glass here and there, especially in hot weather, would suffice. She did use it to swallow a multivitamin and a daily dose of coated, full-strength aspirin. There was cranberry juice or apple juice with meals.

Dinner was pasta and either fish (a fillet of some kind, grilled or sautéed) or meat. Although she didn't eat hamburger, Mama would occasionally make a passable meatloaf. A small portion of sirloin steak could be made pizzaiola-style, sautéed with tomatoes and parsley and a little garlic, or under the oven broiler with a touch of oil and vinegar.

During Mama's later years, a kosher butcher shop opened around the corner from her house. From then on, this devoutly Catholic woman would eat beef—a fillet or a thin, boneless, fatless little steak—or chicken only from that establishment. She claimed it tasted better, and, in a nod to her fastidious nature, believed it was more cleanly handled. (So keen on cleanliness was Mama that she would make excuses not to go to dinner at the homes of ladies who, she felt, kept something less than a spotless kitchen.) Lamb chops probably were Mama's favorite meat, broiled plain in the toaster-oven. She would slice away most of the fat on the corners and eat the rest, down to the bone.

Her teeth remained strong into her nineties. (Her tooth-brushing regimen: baking soda, not toothpaste.)

Mama did have a sweet tooth, but satisfied it with selectivity. Fluffy and gooey layer cakes were not her things; she preferred fruit tarts or ice cream, though she would not touch whipped cream. A little chocolate was always welcome, thank you.

Perhaps it was not curious that Mama should want to impose on us kids the elements of regularity and sameness that she herself practiced. Not a consumer of cereal, for instance, she had heard, or thought she had heard, one or more of us say we liked cornflakes. So, when she shopped for cereal, she invariably brought home cornflakes, a product almost as old as she ("Fat-free and cholesterol-free since 1906," according to Kellogg's publicity machine). To be fair, as new and exotic items began enlarging the supermarket cereal aisles, with their strident claims of enduring health, Mama probably found it easier to choose the familiar package of cornflakes amid the bewildering new selections. Cornflakes, the plain vanilla of cereals, was evidently the favorite in Mama's native country too. On one visit to Italy, where, like Mama, they're not much into cereals, my wife, Christine, and I found only cornflakes as the cereal offered in the breakfast rooms of four hotels.

When it came to jellies, where it should have been easier to make varied selections, Mama invariably brought home grape. To this day, if there are other choices, I do not eat cornflakes or grape jelly, having had my fill of them.

The fabulous dishes of Mama's I came to love in my adult years served to soften the memories of some of the dictatorial and well-meaning but ill-advised methods she used to feed me in earlier years. As a young child, I abhorred breakfast. But as an early gradeschooler, I was made to eat "healthfully." So upon waking, I had to down hard-boiled eggs and large glasses of orange juice and cold milk. Off I went, burping and flatulent to second grade. Much later, on one Saturday just before I went to play on the high school football team, Mama, "for energy," had me eat a large steak, something she herself would never do. That made me the slowest lineman on the field, or made me feel like it. From that time on, pregame meals were less weighty. In the care and feeding of a growing child, Mama's instincts apparently were not as sure as those that informed her own eating habits.

Often, after one of my weekends home from college, Mama would insist on my taking back with me a large globe of provolone cheese, suspended on a cord. I never had the heart to tell her it was not my favorite cheese; most of the time, the smelly prize was devoured by dorm mates.

Hard Work ... and No Car

Mama's way of living bore some of the same trademarks as her eating regimen: simplicity and regularity, to which she added energy.

First of all, there was work—a lot of it, and for a long time. She was a seamstress, as mentioned earlier, and by all accounts the star of the factory. In the days before piecework became politically incorrect, she carried the work home from the factory many blocks away, in bundles that looked as big as she was. (She was barely five feet tall, and never overweight.)

I was no more than seven and remember her working late into the night at the patterned, tin-topped kitchen table in Newark. It was during the Second World War, and as test air-raid sirens signaled a blackout, she would turn on a flashlight and continue to sew. In the morning, she carried the finished garments back to the factory, fast of foot as if the burden didn't exist.

She carried the work because Mama never drove a car in her life. Neither, by the way, did her husband. In America, they lived mostly in urban or close-by suburban settings, with reliable mass transit available. There was plenty of opportunity for exercise of the walking and climbing kind. And neither smoked, so there was wind to spare. In Newark, where we lived during my elementary school years, we had the top apartment in the three-family house we owned, and there was no elevator. (According to the New England Centenarian Study, many centenarians interviewed had lived in second- and third-floor apartments in three-family houses, requiring daily weight-bearing exercise, such as climbing stairs.)

All shopping was done on foot, as well. Then we moved to South Orange, a suburb of Newark, and the stores were more distant. Mama would walk to the center of town, about a mile from the house, zipping along as if exorcising even the thought of idleness. Then she carried back the groceries under her arm. Or, she would walk to the bank, almost as far, to deposit or cash checks. If, after arriving home, she discovered the teller had given her more, or less, money than the check called for, she would walk all the way back to make things right.

As for Mama not driving, all the better, I say. The customary stuffing of a car with massive amounts of groceries from the supermarket would have thrown our home larder into serious imbalance. As the Italians (in Italy) do, better to buy what you need for the night's meal, and maybe one or two in advance. To do that, Mama walked, and that kept her trim all her life.

Mama's lifestyle was defined by her personality and predominant frame of mind.

She was outwardly easygoing and nonconfrontational. If she had some "crosses," she bore them well. The sparks they sometimes caused kept her lively. You'll read about them later; food has a role in the telling.

Then there were the blessings, not crosses, that sustained her, with food also playing a central role. There were the hours-long Sunday dinners with her children and her children's children—all ten grandchildren at times. (When the grandchildren grew up, they produced thirteen great-grandchildren. A pair of twin girls among the latter group, Paige and Sara

Underwood, grandchildren of Alba and her husband, Jim, having heard Papa's description of Mama, named their cat Benigna.) And then there were the feasts Mama would prepare on festive occasions for relatives who came to what was obviously their favorite kitchen venue. And there were the favorite meals she'd make for grandkids just back from college. And the pasta she'd occasionally cook for the lady students from nearby Seton Hall University, to whom she rented rooms in her large Victorian-style house. And the sandwiches she'd make for housepainters, masons, plumbers, or any other vendors who spent any time working in or around the house. My daughter Laura's view is that there was a tie to longevity in this aspect of her grandma—socializing and nurturing people with food and other assistance. I think that's right. The nurturees ran the gamut: children and grandchildren, college students, matronly friends, and, most of all, her increasingly weakening husband, Pasquale, along with his eccentric and frustrated brother-in-law John, and her needy and delusional sister Eleanor, these last three the begetters of Mama's principal crosses.

Elevating Worry to an Art

Among other traits, Mama was a worrier, which is not supposed to be good for you. But it is a trait that threaded through the whole family. Papa watched the television for reports of bad weather. If a storm was close, he would warn us all about the impending *tempesta*, or the feared subsequent flood, which he pronounced "flowed." Mama wrung her hands when any of the three children was about to drive off on snowy roads.

In truth, we siblings are all a little like that, having inherited the worrying gene. So are some of our kids, Mama's grandchildren. The unspoken theory behind it, I believe, is that once the specter of disaster has been invoked, it will never happen. "Don't skid off the road on that tight corner in the park," results, invariably, in no such thing happening. If warnings are not uttered beforehand, who knows what terrible things could befall you or your loved ones.

I sometimes think that, as a family, we were so good at this that if we marketed ourselves as a team of safety experts, we would be as famous as the Wallendas on the trapeze, or the Gruccis, world-renowned for shooting off fireworks for big celebrations. "We're having a presidential inauguration, with millions coming. Hire the Mazzarellas to figure out all the things that can go wrong!" Like the rest of us, Mama survived her worrying habits; evidently, the satisfaction of seeing the beneficial results of the worrying—meaning the nonresults—outweighed the dread of the worrying itself.

There was one time when an attack of worrying caught Mama by surprise and was followed immediately by its resolution. The episode was touched off by a small tragedy, and still makes me wince and smile at the same time. I was in fourth or fifth grade. Crossing the street outside our Newark house, I found my beloved cat, Butch, dead on the curb, victim of a hit-and-run driver. I ran upstairs, threw myself on the living room floor, and sobbed. Mama threw her arms in the air, awaiting the devastating news, sure, she said later, that something had happened to my brother or sister. Finding out it was "just the cat" spared her an immediate emotional collapse and caused her to snap viciously at me for scaring her. She did not have a hard heart when it came to animals. But, forevermore, she maintained that it was a mistake to have any pets whatsoever, because they only produced heartache when they died. Nevertheless, we did have pets, mainly cats, providing Papa a basis of comparison between them and his wife.

In spite of her harsh words, Mama seemed to have a certain affinity with animals. It seemed that if one of our cats was looking for a warm lap for an evening, it was Mama's that it would choose, despite her protests. She affected a dislike for the cats, insisting that they (a) do not know how to stop eating, and (b) draw the breath from babies—that calumny visited upon felines for centuries.

Mama's ambivalence toward animals is best illustrated by a story told by my nephew, Stewart Logan, Alba's eldest son, who, for a time, lived in Mama's house while he was attending Seton Hall University. One day, Mama called him to her bedroom. Outside the window, on the sloped roof over the porch below, sat a raccoon, looking intently through the window. Stewart says Mama smiled and cooed over the "cute" animal. Then she turned to him: "Stew, kill it," she ordered. (He did nothing of the sort; the raccoon ran away.)

Another curious thing is how Mama would describe a particularly handsome dog that somebody might bring around. She would say that the beast *"assomiglia un cristiano,"* meaning it looked human, like a Christian. But why "like a Christian?" In fact, in her generation, it was common to describe a person as a Christian, whether he or she was or not. In Sunday morning coffee klatches, when Italian friends and relatives came to the house for an hour's worth of espresso, anisette, and gossip, you might hear, "The car veered into the crowd and two *cristiani* were killed."

Could it be that ancestral memory going back to the sixteenth century differentiated between ordinary Italians and the Muslim Ottomans who had designs on taking over the Italian peninsula? If you were the former, perhaps, you were automatically a *cristiano*, whether you were an atheist, a Jew, or whatever. In 2009, while my wife, Chris, and I were waiting for a ferry to take us from Terracina, south of Rome, to the island of Ponza, I found that the practice of calling people Christians, indiscriminately, was still alive in Italy more than half a century after I first heard my mother and relatives do it. A white-haired snack vendor at the dock bemoaned the stormy weather, which he said had forced a busload of some one hundred *cristiani* to forgo an earlier crossing.

Mama was a practicing Roman Catholic, walking to Sunday Mass at Our Lady of Sorrows Church in South Orange, a mile or so from home, until very late in life. On quiet afternoons, she could be seen reading her worn missal in the semilit living room. Those readings seemed to grow more frequent the older she got, perhaps, as she contemplated the end. She never uttered a word that showed she feared death, though she spoke of it occasionally, and dismissively. "Nobody lives forever. Good-bye!"

Believing in the force of prayer, Mama made constant church visits beseeching the Lord to help Bud get military draft deferments in the early fifties. He was, in fact, deferred for four straight years, because he worked in what was termed a nationally essential industry: chemicals. The draft board snagged him the fifth year, but by then the Korean War was over.

Mama may have thought her prayers kept Bud out of uniform for those four years; the fact that he was a brilliant chemical engineer with a number of patents to his name, however, may have borne weight along with any intervention by the Lord.

Calling in Her "Boys"

For the most part, Mama was modest and shy (though she always liked to have people around her). But in the house, at least, she was not averse to swearing, sometimes because Papa's complaining was getting to her, sometimes because she thought some tradesman had made her pay too much. "May he spend it all on medicines" was her novel oath in the latter circumstance, issued perhaps with a muttered little expletive (in Italian of course) on the side. (The irony was that, except for these little outbursts, swear words were never heard within the family.)

Once, she and Papa had a dispute with a house painter commissioned to freshen up our new South Orange house. The painter, a tall Greek, sputtered at Mama and Papa, and they sputtered back, he in his thick Greek accent, they in their equally thick southern Italian accents. It was a war of central Mediterranean-flavored words.

Then it looked as if the dispute—whose particulars I do not recall—would turn physical. Our side couldn't offer much in any impending scuffle. I was in my early teens. Bud wasn't home. And Papa putting his dukes up was out of the question, the thought amusing really.

Mama knew what to do. She phoned for her "boys," four street-smart sons of her brother, Crescenzo. Mama had helped to raise the boys—Aldo, Rudy, Joey, and Vince—after their father had died young in the early 1930s. Their mother, the tiny, cherub-cheeked Elisabetta, was often not well. The boys adored Mama and paid her the ultimate compliment an Italian aunt can receive: they called her *zitzi*, a special derivation of the proper word for aunt, *zia*. You could have many *zias* but only one *zitzi*—the favorite one.

The toughest and youngest of the brothers, Vince, also known as Babe, answered his *zitzi*'s call for help. Short, swarthy, and muscular, his body tense, Babe came through the front door with a "What-seems-to-be-the-trouble-here?" swagger. The big house painter, a good foot taller, took one look at the intruder's narrowed eyes, closing fists, and clenched jaw and backed down quickly. The dispute was over. Mama was to outlive all four of the handsome, scrappy brothers, each of whom she had once cradled in her arms.

Most of the time, though, Mama was placid. Whatever else was going on around her in the kitchen, she just kept her head low over the food, workmanlike. Yet there was one time when she enjoyed fifteen minutes of fame—nationally. She was eighty-nine at the time. *Good Morning America* wanted to do a segment on elderly people, long-time empty nesters who chose to remain in their homes with companions. The reporter found two elderly gentlemen, longtime friends, who had moved in together when they became widowers. She poked around South Orange and also found Mama through contacts at Seton Hall University. She learned that Mama had been renting rooms to female students (who, incidentally, had to abide by Mama's ironclad rule: no boys upstairs).

So into Mama's living room one morning marched the reporter and the cameraman and the soundman. Mama sat primly on the edge of the long red couch and, in her broken English, under the lights, told America how nice it was to have the company of the girls and how she would have had to give up the house without them. That last part was a fabrication; the house was paid for. I suppose it was something she thought she was expected to say, or perhaps a poignant storyline she thought the TV newshounds would be delighted to hear. (Another instance of her empathetic ways.) Mama offered the TV crew a little food before they left.

Mama liked television, especially the soaps. When she was well over a hundred, she would pass long, pleasant afternoons in front of the set, absorbed in the interwoven tales of joy and grief. Next to her was her longtime principal caregiver, strong, stout Dina, who helped prepare meals and helped Mama get around on her sometimes painful, once-broken hip.

But all the television watching seemed not to hamper Mama's native mental quickness. She never went beyond elementary school, and learned

English only well enough to get by, but she could ascertain people's thoughts almost to the point of clairvoyance. If something was troubling you, it couldn't be kept for long from Mama.

And when it came to numbers, her brain worked something like a calculator. She added, subtracted, and divided lists of numbers, all in her head; it was said that her mother, who ran the small family shop in Mirabella Eclano, and kept accounts on slips of paper, did the same into her nineties.

Then, several years before Mama entered a nursing home, which happened three months shy of her death, she began suffering from short-term memory loss. The doctors said it wasn't Alzheimer's but could be severe. Yet, even in the nursing home, weak and weary from the effects of pneumonia and old age, she would let Alba ask her to come up with the answers to columns of numbers, all written down, to be added or subtracted. Most of the time, just looking at them, she got the answers right, and quickly.

Because of this faculty of Mama's, it was she, and not Papa, who handled the family's money. I remember once, in the 1940s, Papa came home with his first weekly hundred-dollar pay envelope, the equivalent of around a thousand dollars in today's money. Mama said a few words of appreciation, before the envelope fairly levitated into her quick, little hands.

Laughter unto the Beyond

One trait of Mama's that was clearly healthy was her ability to laugh. Not just giggles or a few *ha-has*, but the paralyzing kind of laughter, when the eyes tear and the nose runs and one gasps seemingly unto apoplexy. It were as if these laughing outbursts served to expel whatever troublesome humors dwelled within her at the time. (Laughter reduces stress hormones and strengthens the immune system, according to some health experts.)

Frequently what touched off this mirthful explosion was some of Papa's self-deprecating humor. Absurd things were always happening to him on his commutes home from Brooklyn, New York, where he was a tailor for the old Howard Clothes Company. Years after his death, the recollection of a funny experience of his would set Mama off.

There was the time a pair of Italian-born ladies didn't like the way he squeezed into an elevator. Speaking Italian and believing he would not understand what they were saying, they agreed with one another that he was a jerk, only to have him turn on them with a few choice words in their common language.

Or the time, weak and weary from the numbing job of sewing in Howard's hot brick building on Flatbush Avenue, he sank into a coveted seat on the No. 5 train rumbling from Brooklyn into Manhattan. From there, he would board another train across the Hudson River into New Jersey, and then take the Newark No. 31 bus home. It was a punishing commute he endured for three decades. As Papa told the story, out of nowhere, two nuns came and stood directly over him as the subway car sped between the boroughs. Papa, responding to what he perceived to be the foot-tapping impatience of one of the nuns, reluctantly gave her his seat, and stood the rest of the way. He bemoaned the sad little episode to us at the table that evening.

"Why did they have to stand right over *me?*" he said. "Poor, tired *me?*"

Mama nearly choked laughing. (Sometimes Papa did other things on his way home from New York, however, that Mama did *not* find humorous, such as buy things, especially little plants or pictures, before Mama could get her hands on his pay.)

Another time, Mama descended into crippling laughter, which continued long after the event, when she watched President George H. W. Bush indignantly defy all nutritionists and tell the world on television of his lifelong hatred of broccoli. His mother had made him eat it when he was a boy, he'd said, followed by, "I'm president of the United States, and I'm not going to eat any more broccoli." Mama found that funny in the extreme.

In the nursing home, Mama kept her sense of humor, kidding the nurses even as they tried, without much success, to get her to eat. Her esophagus had shriveled, and she—this person who was so particular about what she ate—had been put on a baby-food-like diet. My Bolivian barber, Davide, had said that with old people, you knew the end was near when they stopped eating. And so it was. But, between attempted feedings, Mama would manage a mischievous grin, poke a finger into her nurse's ample chest, and promise, "If you help *me*, God will help *you*."

The nurses and God could help Mama only so much. The end came on a sunny January afternoon, in the midst of one of her long naps. These interludes were often interrupted by Mama deliriously calling out for her own mother, whom she had not seen in nearly ninety years. Then, with Alba and Alba's husband, Jim, close by, she suddenly arched her back, raised both arms to the ceiling, and eased back down. Minutes later, still asleep, she stopped breathing, and we lost her.

Mama's Last Contemporaries

A husband, his brother-in-law, a sister—these were the last of Mama's generation within the family, all of whom she amply outlived.

Her interaction with these contemporaries was nuanced. She was a center in their lives, but that presented her with some heavy challenges. Yet those challenges could not outweigh her capacity for affection, or at least forbearance, enjoyed by these last relatives to the end of their days.

Just as Mama's tale has been told, what follows are stories of these three that tell something about their lives and how they benefited from having her in their midst.

Pasquale's Story

Although he never seriously cooked anything—except, occasionally, a sly concoction known as eggs marsala—my father Pasquale Mazzarella exerted a tremendous influence over Mama's kitchen. This was not because of the perfunctory desires he would continually make known: no meal could be called that, he insisted, without a pasta. A glass of wine was a necessity as well. Rather, Papa's influence over Mama's meals was his high blood pressure. He suffered from it for what must have been half his lifetime. Doctor's orders, therefore, dictated that, in addition to being restricted to a small amount of wine at supper, he consume a minimum of salt.

So Mama cooked, and the family ate, food with little salt. For years and years. That must have been good for our collective health. But Papa sometimes reeled under the weight of this cruel medical injunction. When a dish fairly cried out for salt but had none, he would moan, *"Insipido. Insipido!"* (Insipid!) Sometimes, Mama would try to compensate with an extra pinch, touching off the cries of a soul too accustomed to sodium deprivation: *"Salata. Salata!"* (Salty!) To which Mama would sigh, and say, *"Che croce!"* (What a cross!)

Food, insipid or salty, was on two occasions literally a life-saver for Papa. At sixty, he contracted pleurisy. I was home at the time the illness struck and thought he was having a heart attack. At St. Michael's Hospital in downtown Newark, doctors stuck a tube in his back to drain fluid from around his lungs and left him to contemplate his newfound inactivity—and the sheer vileness of the hospital food placed before him.

Rather than see her husband expire from pleurisy, starvation, or both, Mama, with daughter Alba's help, brought homemade food to him daily—pasta, steak pizzaiola, green beans, pastina in broth, and such. He recovered nicely.

One day ten years later, his stomach and chest suddenly became badly swollen. This time it was more serious: cirrhosis of the liver. He was never a serious drinker; I never saw him consume anything alcoholic, except a modest amount of wine with dinner. The doctors' theory was that he had contracted an undiagnosed case of hepatitis as a young man, perhaps when he had fought with the Italian army against the Austrians in the Alps in the First World War. ("Fighting" may be making too much of it. Papa said that, in a week's time, only a few shots would ring out across the snowy valleys.) Although the doctors didn't think alcohol was the cause of the cirrhosis, I questioned, rightly or wrongly, whether the pungent wine he used to make had something to do with it.

In our house in Newark, we had huge presses and barrels in the basement. As a kid, I helped Papa, brother Bud, and an uncle or two make wine with barbera and muscatel grapes imported by the crateful from California. One day after the pressing was done, and as the wine was fermenting in a huge oaken vat, a cork the size of a softball blew off the vat and missed my head by a few inches. It blasted a hole several inches deep in the plaster ceiling. I can imagine the headline had I been in the missile's way: "Twelve-year-old killed by bolt from Italian red."

Much admired by the men, the wine, to me, was suspect. I was sure it was capable of causing gastric distress even in small quantities. I made this view clear as Papa and the elders tried unsuccessfully to get me to drink their wine, alleging it was "good for you." Maybe I was just too young to appreciate it.

Dealing with the cirrhosis, the doctors patched up Papa as best they could in a surgery that lasted many hours. They intoned that he had a few years to live, if that. As it turned out, both his examining doctor and the renowned surgeon who had led the operation died before he did. Papa made it for ten years more, to eighty. It is my belief that, as in the case of his pleurisy ten years earlier, Mama's food, brought with great care to the hospital, helped pull him through. Having no family history pointing to the long-life genes of Mama and the Preziosi womenfolk, Papa needed all the help he could get.

Papa is mainly remembered for his sardonic sense of fun, going back to the long bedtime stories he would make up on the fly for us kids. Then there were the stories he told on himself; he was always the victim of his own or somebody else's stupidity. Like most Mazzarellas, Papa could not carry a tune. But Alba swears she heard him trying to sing a Beatles song ("I Want to Hold Your Hand") after seeing the band on the Ed Sullivan show.

His gentleness did not fit at all with the origin of his surname, which had nothing to do with the cheese (mozzarella). The name's stem, *mazza*, comes from *amazzare*, which means "to kill," or can refer to "mace," the vicious medieval, spiked-ball weapon. The centuries, apparently, had weaned the militarism out of the clan.

Papa presented a somewhat patrician figure. He was just shy of six feet, with a generous nose, hooded hazel eyes that were alternately soulful and sly, and symmetrical frontal balding, which turned bright red in even the earliest summer sun. During his decade of borrowed time after his operation, Papa lost some of the stylish bearing that had been his trademark in earlier years. He seemed to have shrunk and walked with less of a bounce. He no longer spent long hours making dresses for Alba or repairing pants for me.

With all of the children having moved out of the house, Papa would complain that he and Mama were alone, roaming the house like *"due cani"*—two dogs. Maybe he should have had a real dog. He didn't. He did have a come-and-go cat, and a succession of canaries. The birds died one after another, prematurely it seemed, either from fright of the cat or from being overfed by Papa, in which case they would have been both the beneficiaries and victims of the family reverence for food.

Papa wasn't shy about complaining of certain aches and pains, to Mama's dismay. But, though long retired, he still wore a tie most days, and a jacket if he was going out. He had a snappy collection of hats, as well.

There was, in fact, a touch of vanity about the man. Bud remembers that while Papa was recovering from his pleurisy, upon hearing relatives were on their way to see him in the hospital, he quickly donned a shirt and tie under his bathrobe.

Italy? Papa, Si', Mama, No

Papa read a lot, especially the Italian-language newspaper *Il Progresso*, edited and distributed in the United States. His written and spoken Italian was of the proper sort, largely free of the dialect that colored the speech of other Mirabella Eclano townspeople of his generation. Papa didn't attend university, but, as a teenager, had a spell of seminary instruction along with his cousin, Bernardino Mazzarella, who went on to become a Franciscan bishop in Honduras.

The truth is that Papa was sentimentally tied to the old country. Every so often, when American produce seemed anemic to him, he'd brag about the robust fruits he remembered from the old country. In his memory, plums and peaches were as big as baseballs, heads of lettuce as big as soccer balls. "Uh huh," we said.

In the years following the Second World War, Papa and Mama sent packages to family members left in Italy. This eased the difficult times these relatives were going through. But also, I felt, these shipments permitted Papa to hold onto a sentimental attachment to the land of his youth, with its miraculous orchards, amid other wonders. It was an embrace by parcel post.

Papa would carefully stitch white cloth around large boxes and write the address in Italy directly on the cloth in black ink. Then he would lug them to the post office on foot. My parents surely did not fit the legendary "rich American relative" myth. Mama and Papa were not rich, by any means. Both had held onto decent, though moderately paying, jobs through the Depression and even managed to buy a three-family house on Twelfth Street in Newark in 1940. They could afford to send clothes and other necessities, such as over-the-counter medicines and cosmetics, to brothers, sisters, nephews, and nieces in Mirabella Eclano.

Looking through some old photographs, I found a touching letter sent from Italy to dear *Zio* (Uncle) Pasquale by one his young nieces, Giuseppina, in March 1953. "Even the poorest girls in town try to dress well," she wrote, "with painted lips and rouge. We young ones cannot make a *brutta figura* [bad impression], and we have not done so, thanks to your help." She was alluding to whatever clothes or cosmetics she had received in the packages.

It wasn't a one-way flow. The relatives in Italy would send us their own prized goods, including cheeses and olive oil. One particularly welcome import was a gourd of medium-firm cheese, covered in a thin coating of wax and with pure butter at its core.

In time, the relatives in Italy prospered, and my parents stopped sending care packages. They resumed the practice when I and my own family moved to Rome for work in 1966. We didn't need clothes, but we could use other things. On top of the list was toilet paper, which in those days in Italy had not fully made the transition from wood to paper. Mama and Papa happily sent us these items and others.

They came to Italy to visit us. Papa was in his glory. He went for long walks, taking in the sweet Roman air. He bought himself a fine Italian fedora. He pointed with pride to the apartment he had rented for a short time after the war in a now-exclusive building in the trendy Piazza Navona.

Not long after those carefree Rome days as a young bachelor, Papa emigrated to America. He was the third youngest in a large brood of brothers and sisters. Mama was the youngest child in her family. The two were raised in the same village, Mirabella Eclano. Both were the children of shopkeepers. Though just two years apart, they apparently were not that close in the old country. Mama had a dashing boyfriend, a certain Alessio; Papa reportedly made eyes at one of Mama's sisters, the once-trim Eleanor. It was only in the teeming immigrant circles of Brooklyn, New York, and Newark, New Jersey, that Mama and Papa got together.

Inspired by his trips to see us in Rome, in his late middle age, Papa would have been content, I am sure, to spend the rest of his days in Italy, sampling all the pastas and fresh grilled fishes. Mama, by contrast, found her return to Italy unsatisfying. On a visit to the old hometown, she was shocked to find that Alessio, the one-time boyfriend with whom she had ridden on a motorcycle as a teenager, was now a scraggly pensioner, missing most of his teeth. She didn't like the flies, either, and she wasn't crazy about the food, except for the *abbacchio*, broiled baby lamb, which must have reminded her of her succulent lamb chops back in the States.

Returning from such visits, Papa would settle into his routine of doing a little tailoring work in retirement, reading, and watching television. Mama noted that he would especially perk up if there was a chorus line or some other display of female legs on television, or if it was time for the Loretta Young show. That mid-twentieth-century actress was Papa's ideal of female beauty, charm, and sophistication, and he never missed her show.

How differently he would regard Mama when she was guilty of that little nighttime trick of hers, sneaking her little foot into his pants pocket as he dozed on cold evenings. A muffled laugh that barely broke through Mama's teeth was her response to his ire upon awakening.

Mama's relationship with Papa, during the last decades of their fifty-one-year marriage, seemed to be a mixture of exasperation, solicitousness, and love—the love not being of the most demonstrative kind. In the later years, after his operations, Mama was sometimes abrupt with him, saying things such as, "*Basta* (Enough) with the complaining!" (He kept insisting he had a sharp pain in his ribs, despite being told nothing could be found to cause it.) Eventually, the cirrhosis finished him. He got to the hospital just in time to die.

Mama was demonstrative enough at his wake, weeping openly in a way that surprised some who didn't know she had that kind of emotion in her. She remarked through tears how *bello* (handsome) Papa looked in the casket, laid out in his favorite brown suit, his old horned-rim glasses fixed on his nose. Until that day, I had never seen Mama cry, expending the same amount of energy with which she laughed.

Into advanced age, Papa never lost his appetite, and he would make specific culinary requests. Homemade pasta was one. And there were two others, in particular. Neither aroused my tastes as a boy, though I warmed to them later. They were as follows:

1. Spaghetti or linguine aglio, olio, e peperoncino (spaghetti or linguine with garlic, oil, and hot pepper flakes).
2. Baccalà (dried and salted cod fish), poached, with olive oil and lemon.

The strength of flavors in these dishes made it unnecessary to have much salt in either, so the blood pressure was kept in check. (Recipes for both are in the book.)

There is one other thing to report about Papa's eating habits, and one, alas, that I inherited: he was a spiller. Of various table bits, juices, and even wine. This last accident was considered "good luck," though not by Mama. Sugar proved especially tricky. Papa would spoon it and carry it shakily to his cup, spilling some over the distance. Mama yelled at him every time he did this.

Now, years after Papa's death, I, and some others close to me, whenever something spills on the table or on clothes during a meal, sense a certain spiritual presence: "Pasquale is here," one of us will say.

Uncle John's Story

For Mama, the pasta course was an introduction to the rest of the meal—there was always a *secondo*, or second dish—and, as such, was subject to some reserve. No heaping mounds of pasta for the first dish, such as you find in some of America's family-style Italian restaurants. There was one exception to this rule, however, and that had to do with Uncle John.

Mama always piled his plate high, and this was true not only of the pasta, but of whatever came afterward. This may have seemed strange, inasmuch as Mama had a considerable aversion to Uncle John. From Papa's side, he entered the family's most intimate circle for a number of years, causing Mama no small amount of irritation. But she did the right thing—families engender responsibilities, after all—and took care of him as she did everybody else.

John Cifelli was a trim, short barber who had married my father's sister, Aunt Adeline, in the 1930s, after she and John had emigrated to America. She was a tall, hawk-like woman who was the undisputed matriarch of the clan (although she had no children of her own). She instilled fear in some relatives and children of relatives. John she treated like a nice puppy, and he, in turn, acted like one in her regard. They were a Mutt and Jeff couple. Adeline died in late middle age from kidney disease, a Mazzarella curse, or so the family mythology held.

Despite his subservience to Adeline, and his totally wimpish persona—squinting eyes, gray hair sticking up like a ridiculous crew cut, and a droning voice given to giggles—Uncle John was somewhat of a ladies' man, or more precisely, a man who liked to have a lady around. He married a second time, to an ancient-looking woman called Antoinette, who treated him with the same mixture of condescension and affection that Adeline had.

But she died too, and John again was alone. He then quietly inquired whether Aunt Eleanor, who had long been widowed, might be available for a late-in-life betrothal. Mama, Eleanor's sister, flew into a rage at this prospect and, I believe, even prevented the overture from getting to Eleanor, who, if she had heard it, probably would have laughed down a shot or two of whiskey.

This plot having failed, there was no one to take care of Uncle John, now in his seventies. So, for the rest of his days, he lived with us in the old Victorian-style house on Fairview Avenue in South Orange. He didn't exactly *live* with us. He took his meals with us, though, and spent most of his waking hours in our house.

But Mama would not hear of his sleeping in the house, even though it would have been possible to fix up the threadbare bedroom in the attic for him. Mama decreed that John should rent a room across the street, but could have his meals and socialize with us in our house. Moreover, he was told his bathroom was not one of the two upstairs, but the one in the dingy basement. Uncle John complied without complaint.

I'm not sure what it was about Uncle John that rankled Mama so. It may have been his general creepiness. He talked a lot for a solitary man; perhaps, he talked a lot because he was solitary. He would bend Papa's ear on subjects he felt strongly about. Some things were *"magnifico"* to him. For example, the tenor at the Metropolitan Opera performance that both of them had taken the train to Manhattan to see (standing in the back of the orchestra). Or, the wine on a given evening. (Uncle John had been a co-conspirator in the home wine works in the Newark house years before, bestowing *"magnifico"* on what I thought were foul batches of the white and red. Sometimes, he would even pronounce a wine *"dolce,"* or sweet, apparently the ultimate compliment.) Or, *"magnifico,"* for him, might simply have been Mama's plate of fusilli.

He would also often rant about something or somebody bothering him in the news or in life. I would overhear snippets, such as "... and there are those who do not know the meaning of decent behavior." I got the impression that some of these denunciations were obliquely aimed at a cousin of his, the suave, mustache-twirling Uncle Vitaliano. This debonair fellow, also a barber, had married another sister of Papa's, Leondina, a tall redhead.

The contrasts between the cousins were stark in the extreme. John shuffled through life; Vitaliano bounded through it. In his younger days, Vitaliano had been a mandolin-strumming vaudeville performer. I remember seeing pictures of him in the spotlight, resplendent in a white suit. Vitaliano, too, had strong opinions: the Yankees were the real bums, though "I always want to see DiMaggio do well." Perversely, John said he was a Dodgers fan, though I am sure he knew little or nothing about baseball.

Vitaliano had married Leondina, a stately beauty, and together they had four handsome children, two boys and two girls. John had married a stately but plain woman, and they had no children. (Adeline did sort of adopt us kids, however; Alba was her favorite.) There was plenty about Vitaliano that could cause anguish and envy in John.

So it could be that Mama, while barely holding back her distaste of him, tolerated Uncle John's pervasive presence, in part, because she also felt sorry for him.

Uncle John and the Cat

But, on the negative side, maybe Mama took offense at something the rest of us observed with amusement—Uncle John's contradictions. He seemed meek, solicitous, and generous: children and grandchildren could expect a dollar or two to be slipped into their hands from his. And yet there was an edgier strain in the man. Every Sunday, he would cut the menfolks' hair in the sunny upstairs bathroom (the only time he was allowed in), and no amount of pleading could dissuade him from cutting the hair exactly as he wanted, his rubbery hands turning to steel on one's skull as he snipped away with the hurtful manual clipper.

Then there was his schizophrenic behavior toward the cat. With others present, Uncle John would bestow compliments upon him, such as, *"Un bel gatto!"* (A beautiful cat!) Alas, whenever the cat inadvertently invaded his space, and Uncle John thought no one was looking, he would register a quick kick on the animal with his dwarf-like foot. *Pow!* Right in the whiskers. Hearing a yelp in the next room, we knew Pussy had felt Uncle John's fleeting wrath.

Another peculiarity about Uncle John was that he was virtually never sick. He had one run-in with an unruly prostate, but that was fixed with one day in the hospital. I once asked around in the family: no one had seen Uncle John suffer from anything else, not even a cold. He may have had a chance to outlive Mama if it were not for the accident. It had happened on South Orange Avenue in Newark, not far from the barber shop he worked in long after conventional retirement. A car hit him. He landed on his head, but showed relatively little effect from it. Everybody wondered how he had lived through it. But the blow apparently scrambled something. Not long after, he had to be admitted to a nursing home, where he fell into progressive dementia and died.

If a capacity for shrewdness is useful in navigating life's shoals, then Mama profited from possessing that faculty. An example is the way she steered Uncle John to will his savings, several tens of thousands of dollars, to her and Papa, lest somebody else might be planning to plant a stake. She deserved it, after all, having put up with the *croce* of caring for him all those years. This apparently was the view as well of Uncle John, who did not demur, once it became clear he wasn't going to acquire a third wife on whom to spend the money, or to whom to leave it upon his demise.

During Uncle John's lifetime, Mama did find a use for him, notwithstanding the coolness with which she held him. Perhaps, she loaded him down with food in part to keep him quiet; more likely, she used him to get rid of the food that would wind up as leftovers. She was not big on leftovers, and at the same time didn't like to throw food away. (As children, we had to kiss any piece of stale bread that was about to be ditched; one had to think of the poor.)

So Uncle John, nightly, was the last to get up from table, systematically working his way through the spaghetti, the veal or fried fish, the green beans, the devil's food cake—whatever the night's supper might comprise.

Mama had found a use for him: Uncle John drew the task of consuming all the food she would otherwise have had to throw away.

Aunt Eleanor's Story

A unt Eleanor was two years older than Mama. But the sisters were ages apart in everything but their height (in the five-foot range), and the smooth, varicose- and cellulite-free condition of their legs, even into their nineties. Mama was petite, energetic, and steeped in reality. She ate with discipline and sobriety. Aunt Eleanor was rotund, slow of foot, happy-go-lucky, and occasionally heard voices speaking directly to her from the television. She ate—and drank—with abandon.

At least that is how I saw the sisters most of my life. It was not always so. They had been more evenly matched, at least physically, in their youth. It was said, in fact, that in their hometown of Mirabella Eclano, my father had sought the favor of Eleanor more than of Benigna, with whom he linked up only in America.

The sisters arrived together at Ellis Island during the winter of 1920, aboard the Italian steamship *Roma*, on third-class accommodations. They were stuck on the island for a month because of a smallpox scare, though that virus likely would have met its match with this hardy pair. As they sunbathed on high during the quarantine, their brothers, Crescenzo and Domenico, having emigrated earlier and set up business in Newark, shouted encouragement to them from a rowboat below.

It's hard to tell how and when the two sisters began to diverge in habit and appearance. They never diverged in their reciprocal devotion, or in longevity. Eleanor suffered tragedies, and they may have altered her path through life. One of her twin baby girls died at birth. (The other, Dolly, survived, married, and had children, but moved across the country when her mother, in advanced age, needed her most.) A son, Romeo, a tail gunner in the Second World War, was killed when his plane crashed. A short time later, Aunt Eleanor became a widow, at middle age. She never remarried. Her other son, Mikey, a smart guy, never married and worked only long enough at the post office or at the airport to make an amount of money sufficient to enable his gambling compulsion.

Although her table habits may have been influenced by the wrongs fate had dealt her, Aunt Eleanor was not a despondent or depressed person, at least outwardly. I remember her mostly in a good mood, especially if a cold beer was being opened for her on a hot day.

I do not have any recipes of Aunt Eleanor's, and if I did, I probably would not share them. Her fare was, in a word, heavy, the opposite of Mama's. She loved meats of all kind, in thick gravies or fried, roasted, or grilled. At family gatherings, when she couldn't come but Mikey could, she ordered him to bring back a good piece of "that nice grilled steak."

Her pasta portions were large, where Mama's were measured. There were other foods she savored: she would sit with a large basket of tomato-sauced snails on her lap, transferring the succulent little creatures to her mouth with a toothpick. In the late fifties, Mama, Papa, and Aunt Eleanor decided to return to the old country for a vacation. According to Bud, who saw them off, Eleanor had put a loaf of bread under her coat, unsure that the airline would provide sufficient food for the flight.

While Mama abstained from any alcohol whatsoever, Aunt Eleanor liked her red wine, cold beer, and rye whiskey. Mama had to be coaxed to taste even a touch of hot peppers; Aunt Eleanor munched them with glee.

As time went on, Aunt Eleanor was beset with various maladies. None of them was life-threatening, at least into her nineties. But she moved ever more slowly and, worst of all, she had what must have been a botched cataract operation. Her sight was impaired as a result. Going into or out of a house, two strong men had to be on either side of her as she poked a toe, still dainty despite her wide girth, onto the next step or square of pavement.

As time went on, Aunt Eleanor relied more and more on Mama. This is because, in families like theirs, the younger must take care of the older. Sons and daughters take care of parents; younger siblings take care of older ones. So whenever Aunt Eleanor needed something, anything, she called Mama. She would give Mama a shopping list for the supermarket, specifying, "No cheap cuts of the meat, please." Mama would have to have my brother Bud drive her to the store, and then to Aunt Eleanor's with the bags.

Aunt Eleanor and the Six O'Clock News

Then there were the phone calls, at all hours, to Mama. Aunt Eleanor swore they were talking about her on Eyewitness News. Mama listened to her fears and sighed. Often, the phone conversations turned to Mikey. What would happen to her son after she was gone, Aunt Eleanor continually asked.

Mikey always lived at home. When he got some time off from sorting letters or moving airport cargo, he headed for one of the New Jersey raceways, Freehold or Atlantic City, or to Vegas. He was said to have been streetwise with money, shifting cash among bank accounts in a sort of Ponzi scheme involving only himself. It's as if he were both the swindler and the victim.

He was short and wiry, a lightweight boxing champion in one of Roosevelt's largest western conservation corps camps in the 1930s. When I knew him, he was always well-groomed, with tie and jacket, and clear-rimmed glasses. His skin was so smooth that, at seventy, he could pass for fifty. I asked him once if he had a girlfriend. That's when I discovered that he didn't refer to females, plural, as women. The term he used was woman, singular, as in "there is a time for woman …" Apparently, he had compartmentalized elements of his life in a generic way: cash, food, woman, and so on.

Mikey occasionally would impart one of his self-arrived-at truths: most best-of-seven-game championship series in any sport tend to go to 3–3 because "they need the crowds as the series stretches out; they need the dough." Once, as a boy, I asked him why he was smoking on such a hot day. His laconic reply: "Cigarettes. They make you feel cool on a hot day and warm on a cold day," this said in a world-weary way, his voice trailing off. Years later, I found his theory to be, well, strangely true, of my Lucky Strikes.

And, most poignantly, Mikey would sometimes articulate the biggest fear and yet psychological need of the habitual gambler—losing. "I gamble because I have to lose ... have to lose," he'd sigh.

Win or lose, he was a generous soul, like so many in the family. The children of his cousins always got a few dollars stuffed into their hands at birthday parties. Mikey was my godfather at my Roman Catholic confirmation. Walking back from the church, he slipped a ten-dollar bill into my pocket, wordlessly. It was a good bit of money then for a seventh-grader.

At my mother's table, Mikey served, more or less, the same function as Uncle John. He ate whatever was put in front of him, in great quantities (so Mama wouldn't have to save anything). I can still picture him, his mouth full and cheeks puffed out like a squirrel, lost in thought—why had he put it all on that nag in the seventh?

During the phone calls with Aunt Eleanor, Mama would have to reassure her sister that Mikey would be okay after her passing, just as she had to reassure her that the broadcaster really wasn't saying that the police were coming after her, Eleanor Crecco, for some unknown crime. The phone conversations invariably ended with Mama begging off because "I have something on the stove."

"*Che croce,*" Mama would mutter on the way back. "What a cross."

Eventually, Aunt Eleanor was persuaded to move to Las Vegas to live with her daughter Dolly. A short time later, Aunt Eleanor died. She had miraculously survived several operations, but her genes finally gave in to a wrecked stomach. Mikey, who had disparaged his mother at every opportunity ("She does nothing.") nonetheless followed her to Vegas. He died almost exactly a year after she did, of kidney failure and, probably, loneliness. He had spent the year, we were told, living the life of a hermit, letting his once well-trimmed hair grow to his shoulders. Aunt Eleanor's question about Mikey had been answered.

After word got back that Aunt Eleanor had died, Mama reacted similarly to the way she reacted when, nearly a half-century earlier, she had gotten the phone call from Italy telling her that her mother, whom at that time she had not seen in more than thirty years, had died. I have a vision of Mama, standing over the stove, slowly stirring something with one hand, and silently dabbing her nose and eyes with a white handkerchief in the other.

And So ...

Mama bade farewell to the last three family members of her generation—her husband, Pasquale, his brother-in-law John, and her sister Eleanor—grieving for them in her own way as they died. Grieving even, I believe, for the irritating John.

An interesting transition lay ahead. Those last contemporaries had depended on her, the strong Benigna. She had done what she could for them, withstanding the challenges each imposed. Through it all, she had taken responsibility as the sometimes tough-love caregiver. She had been the glue that held the last of her generation together.

Now things were changing. The three family members she had buried had all been older than Mama, and, therefore, she was the one expected to provide support to them. Now, everyone in her life, at least in the extended family and among lady friends who came for tea, was younger. They did not need her daily attention. They simply honored and pampered her, the seemingly everlasting matriarch.

And so, as the years went by in this new era, Mama became more relaxed, no longer weighed down with worry about Pasquale, John, and Eleanor. She even became a bit submissive, allowing others to set the agenda. That especially included my sister Alba, who took Mama into her home on the weekends when the lady hired to help Mama in her own home was off.

Yet even until about her hundredth year, Mama remained the star of the kitchen, distributing her specialties to the children, grandchildren, and great-grandchildren. These younger generations soaked it all in—sauces perfectly balanced and smooth, tasty and always lean chicken, veal and fish, never-too-sweet desserts. And though Mama's catchphrase was "Always eat the hard crust of the bread," the younger kids loved to eat whole slices of the crunchy Italian bread at her house slathered with butter.

Then that era ended, as well. Neither Mama's genes, her catlike luck, nor her willpower could overcome the final challenge of old age. She died in her eleventh decade, leaving behind the memory of her grit, occasional sauciness, disarming laughter, and favorite dishes. Recipes for those dishes and others follow—her legacy to her survivors.

Benigna Preziosi Mazzarella, at ninety-nine, attending the wedding dinner of her son, the author, and Christine Wells in Washington, DC, December 28, 1999.

Benigna, sometime after her arrival in America in 1920, pictured with her brother Crescenzo in front of his store in Newark, New Jersey.

Benigna, looking perky in the 1920s, about the time she was being courted by her future husband, Pasquale Mazzarella.

Pasquale and Benigna at their wedding in 1927. Her two brothers are on the left. The children are a niece and nephew of the couple's. The maid of honor is unidentified.

Mama at middle age, her eyes conveying some of the
steeliness that lay below a soft exterior.

The author and Mama, about ninety, working on a dish
together in her South Orange, New Jersey, kitchen.

The four Preziosi boys, whom Mama helped raise after their father, her brother, died young. From left, Joey, Aldo, Rudy, and Vince ("Babe"). It was Vince who answered Mama's call to intimidate a troublesome house painter. The boys are seen with their mother, the often-ill Elisabetta. Mama outlived all the brothers.

Mama at her one-hundredth birthday party, with a cutout of
her in her twenties, flapper-like, in the background.

Chris sitting between Mama, left, and Chris's mother, Mary Nichols. Also one
with good habits (she was a senior Olympian), Mary lived to ninety-four.

Mama's one hundred and fourth birthday. Author is at
left, with siblings Alba and Emil ("Bud").

Mama's one hundred seventh birthday. She died nine months later.

Giuseppina Scala Preziosi, Mama's mother, pictured late in life. She died at ninety-five in Mirabella Eclano, Italy. Mama, while dying, repeatedly called out to her.

Papa, ever the clothes horse, pictured in a new coat in South Orange, circa 1960.

This semi-candid shot captured a truth of Mama and Papa's marriage: she complained a lot about his complaining, but she also found him very funny.

The couple relaxing in Venice after visiting the author and family in Rome. Note Papa's attire for casual touring: suit and tie.

Uncle John (Cifelli) and Adeline Mazzarella, Papa's sister, on their marriage day in Newark in the 1920s. Mama, on the right, was maid of honor. The groom was to become one of her *"croci,"* or crosses, in later years.

A walk in the city, sometime in the early thirties:
Uncle John, Papa, Alba, and Adeline.

Mama, a preadolescent Alba, and the imposing Adeline who,
though childless, functioned as the matriarch of the extended family
in Newark for several decades. Papa made Alba's dress.

Aunt Eleanor and Mama, middle-aged matrons. Their lives were entwined,
with Mama in the long-suffering support role. Her love for her sister
surpassed the frustration she sometimes felt over Eleanor's eccentric ways.

Aunt Eleanor in one of her typical happy-go-lucky moods.

A classical rendering of *Mentha pulegium*, the scientific name for what the author's family on both sides of the Atlantic called *pullia*. Its English name is *pennyroyal*, the essential ingredient in one of Mama's prized pasta dishes.

Giuseppina Mazzarella, octogenarian cousin of the author, opening a large package of *pullia* that had just been delivered to her home in Mirabella Eclano. Her brother, Emiliano, is at center, and the author is at left.

A boxful of *pullia* drying in the stairwell of the Unaway Hotel in Mirabella Eclano, in preparation for its being brought to America in carry-on luggage.

Part II:
Recipes

APPETIZERS

Bruschetta with Truffle Oil

I don't recall offering this treat to Mama; maybe she would have found it a little too fancy, yet the homey flavors would have appealed to her. It's natural and simple to make, if a little pricey as traditional bruschetta ingredients go. I've written this for a serving of one. Multiply it for as many pieces as you like.

INGREDIENTS

A thick slice of crusty Italian bread, such as casareccia (Also try pita or, better yet, an Iranian flatbread called *taftoon,* crispy and sesame-seed-covered.)

Olive oil infused with white truffle oil, found in higher-end food stores

Imported emmenthaler cheese, sliced by hand from a wedge, not machine-sliced; slices should be thin but not paper-thin

Salt and pepper

¼ teaspoon dried rosemary leaves

PREPARATION

Toast the bread (or pita or taftoon) lightly. Remove it from the toaster and sprinkle a few drops of the truffle oil on it. Lay the cheese on the bread in one layer, so that the whole surface is covered with it.

Add salt and pepper lightly to the cheese, then cover lightly with the rosemary leaves.

Sprinkle the truffle oil over the cheese and rosemary, several drops on each quadrant of the bruschetta.

Place the bruschetta under a broiler just long enough for the cheese to melt, about a minute or two, and serve immediately.

Ricotta Boats

This appetizer is pretty to look at, and every ingredient, except for salt and pepper, is identifiably Italianate. Again, the directions are for one piece; replicate for as many servings as you wish.

INGREDIENTS

A relatively narrow but thick piece of ciabatta bread, with a heavy crust

A couple of tablespoons of ricotta cheese

½ of a plum tomato, sliced

Salt and pepper to taste

Two large basil leaves

Extra virgin olive oil for drizzling

PREPARATION

Toast the bread until it turns brown. Spread the ricotta evenly over the bread, and place the tomato slices on top of it.

Sprinkle salt and pepper over the slices, and follow with the basil leaves. Drizzle the "boat" with olive oil and serve while the bread is still warm.

Hot and Hearty Portuguese Shrimp

This is a fine appetizer, but probably not one best served in a formal setting. It's eaten with the hands, which become pretty slick after shelling big juicy shrimp dripping in oil, wine, and lemon juice, not to mention hot pepper and garlic. So it's better as a starter at a homey barbecue or such (or maybe even the top attraction). The messy routine is worth it. The shrimp have an incredible flavor, evoking the shores of Portugal. In various versions, these spicy shrimp were among my very favorite dishes during the year I spent in Portugal. This particular recipe is lighter on the garlic and hot pepper than the ones used by the Portuguese. Break out the finger bowls and go heavy on the napkins.

INGREDIENTS

3 tablespoons extra virgin olive oil

3 cloves garlic, minced

1 heaping teaspoon hot red-pepper flakes

Juice of one lemon

⅓ cup dry white wine

⅓ cup clam juice

1 pound large or jumbo shrimp, heads off, tails and shells on

1 teaspoon sea salt

1 teaspoon minced dill if fresh, ½ teaspoon if dried

2 tablespoons fresh parsley, coarsely chopped

Toasted Italian bread

PREPARATION

Heat the oil in a large sauté pan until it starts to simmer. Add the garlic and hot pepper, and shake them around. Add the lemon juice, the wine, and the clam sauce and bring the mixture to a boil.

With the heat still high, add the shrimp and sprinkle with the salt and dill. Toss the shrimp quickly, turning them once or twice. The liquid should remain at a boil. The shrimp are done when they turn bright pink on all sides. That should take 4 to 6 minutes, depending on the size of the shrimp. Add the parsley and toss again, then serve hot. Give everybody a large slice of toasted Italian bread to soak up the now-reduced and piquant sauce.

Serves 4

PASTA AND RICE DISHES

(Unless otherwise noted, pasta recipes are intended as first courses)

Mama's Smooth Tomato Sauce, with Spaghetti

The most basic of basics in Mama's kitchen was tomato sauce, for any dish that needed it: most pasta and rice dishes, meat gravies, bruschetta, pizza, eggplant or zucchini parmigiana.

There are as many recipes for tomato sauce in this world as there are Italian mamas. Each one is suited to the tastes of the creator and the family she feeds. In Mama's case, her tastes ran, first of all, to tomatoes without skins or seeds. Not only that, but she preferred the tomatoes to be in the form of a smooth purée, not chunky.

Every year, Mama and her lady friends, to assure they would have enough of the precious purée to last for many dinners, would buy bushel upon bushel of plum tomatoes in late summer or early fall (the best season for them). To help ripening, Mama would spread her ample allotment on newspapers on the sunny back porch for a few days. Then the ladies would gather at one of their homes. At the ready were the hundreds of tomatoes, clean Mason jars, and a powerful electric tomato strainer—a machine that squeezes out the juice and unblemished pulp of the fruit while discarding skin and seeds.

There was a division of labor among the ladies. Someone was in charge of piling the tomatoes into the voracious machine; someone was ready to remove the purée and, on the other side of the device, the skins and seeds; someone had to boil the jars, and so on. Mama, especially in her later years, was in charge of wiping the rim of the jars clean with a cloth before the vacuum jar tops were applied. This fit well with her penchant for cleanliness.

All this resulted in each matron taking home dozens of jars of simple tomato purée, enhanced only by a pinch of salt and a large leaf or two of basil. The purée lasted through the better part of the winter, and Mama always had some jars left over to be given to me, Alba, or Bud when we came to visit.

I wondered whether skinning and seeding the tomatoes for purée detracted from their nutritional value. A 2004 study by New Zealand researchers found that removing skins and seeds created a "significant loss of antioxidants" in the tomatoes. But another study, cited by health.learninginfo.org, found that a group of healthy women experienced a decrease of 33 percent to 42 percent in oxidative cell damage after eating two ounces of tomato purée (no skins or seeds) daily for three weeks, compared with a three-week period in which they followed a tomato-free diet.

Finally, a recipe on the website Life123.com states bluntly, "skins are tough and do not cook well…. They do not add anything to the product and therefore will not be missed." Mama and her lady friends obviously held to this view, a prime motive for them, I believe, being the issue of digestibility.

Whatever the rationale for the purée, it is the essential ingredient of the sauce. The easy way is to look for it ready-made. Most well-stocked Italian food markets, and some of the better general groceries, such as Whole Foods, carry it. The product should be imported from Italy. A good and well-known brand is Pomi, available in 26.5-ounce, brick-shaped cartons, labeled "Strained Tomatoes." Another brand, also available in cartons, is Mutti. There are imported bottled brands as well, including Buonaturae.

If you prefer the homemade version of purée, you can make it with one of those fancy electric machines and put up many jars containing the fruits of your labor, just as Mama and her lady friends did. Or, you can buy a small strainer and make the purée as you need it—one or two meals at a time. That's what I do, with a forty-dollar strainer powered by a hand crank. That modest model, and motorized machines capable of making pounds of purée at a time, costing upward of five hundred dollars, are available on the Web. Try creativecookware.com, and use the link for "Tomato Strainers." (You can also buy one of the cone-shaped strainers, operated with a tapered wooden implement and considerable arm power. That's how, as a boy, my brother Bud puréed the tomatoes for Mama in the early days. I don't recommend it, unless you need the exercise.)

Seasonality is an issue for some, insofar as the tomatoes are concerned. There are those who simply do not make sauce with tomatoes from late fall through winter, considering them bland. In that period, they prefer store-bought, processed tomatoes, such as the purées mentioned above or those large cans of peeled tomatoes—pomodori pelati—imported from Italy (preferably using San Marzano tomatoes).

Whether you strain and bottle tomatoes massively, as Mama and her friends used to do, or prefer to plop a dozen of them in a little crank-spun machine for that night's ration of spaghetti, here are the simple steps:

1. Boil the tomatoes for 10 seconds or so. Drain and douse them with cold water. Cut the tomatoes crossways in half, if they are small, and in thirds if they are large.
2. Place the chunks in the strainer's top basket, the number of chunks depending on the size of the basket, and grind away. With small strainers, you'll want to pass the expelled skin-and-seed pulp through twice.
3. Put the resulting purée in a saucepan with a little salt and let it bubble on the stove over medium-low heat until the purée begins to thicken, 20 to 25 minutes.

Now you're ready to fill the jars (following the jar manufacturer's directions for hygiene), or, if you used just a few tomatoes and the small machine, proceed right to the sauce.

INGREDIENTS

2 tablespoons extra virgin olive oil

¼ red or orange sweet bell pepper, chopped fine

2 garlic cloves (whole)

¼ teaspoon hot red-pepper flakes

¼ sweet onion, chopped fine

2 cups tomato purée (homemade or bought)

1 8-ounce can plain tomato sauce, such as Del Monte or Hunt's

½ teaspoon salt

1 tablespoon tomato paste (if needed)

3 or 4 basil leaves

12 ounces good imported spaghetti or linguine

Grated cheese, preferably Pecorino Romano for this dish

PREPARATION

Warm the olive oil in a large saucepan or sauté pan. Add the chopped bell pepper. Sauté over low heat until the pepper turns soft and pinkish, about 10 minutes.

Add the garlic, the hot pepper flakes, and the onion, and sauté until both the onion and pepper become wilted and translucent, another 10 minutes or more.

The onion and bell pepper should be well-reduced, offering little more than a tantalizing hint of their flavors and texture to the finished sauce. If you prefer tomatoes unadorned, you can eliminate the pepper and onion altogether.

Add the tomato purée, the canned Del Monte or Hunt's sauce, and the salt. Simmer uncovered over medium-low heat until the mixture is reduced and most of the water has evaporated. Mama liked the Del Monte or Hunt's sauces because they were smooth and only slightly spiced, and they added some thickness to her own purée.

The simmering can take a long time if the purée is homemade, depending on how juicy the tomatoes were when strained. If the sauce seems watery, add a tablespoon of tomato paste. Stir occasionally, removing the garlic cloves before they fall apart. (Mama's usual practice.)

When the sauce clings snugly to a wooden spoon, the sauce is ready. Tear up the basil leaves and stir them in.

Cook the spaghetti or linguine in lightly salted boiling water for 1 minute less than the package suggests (for *al dente* consistency). Drain the pasta and mix with the sauce and a light dusting of pecorino cheese. The more noble Parmigiano Reggiano can be used instead, but this dish seems to call for a slightly sharper cheese. The pecorino's tanginess also means less salt can be used in the sauce and pasta water.

Serves 4

"IN THE SPIRIT" OF MAMA

Here's a variation. It doesn't call for purée, but honors the simplicity and naturalness of Mama's sauces, and takes much less time.

Take a dozen or so plum tomatoes, or ripe ordinary tomatoes, boil them as above and remove their skins. Slice them lengthwise in quarters and remove the seeds and the tough white membrane with your fingers. Then slice the quarters into strips a quarter-inch wide.

Sauté the garlic and hot red-pepper flakes (with or without the onion and bell pepper as in the above recipe). Add the tomatoes and bring to a quick boil. Simmer over medium-high heat until the tomatoes are lumpy and the water is mostly evaporated.

Add the salt and a small can of the commercial plain sauce, or a little tomato paste if the mixture is too watery. Toward the end, add a few torn basil leaves.

Now onto some of Mama's other pasta recipes, along with further variations that capture the spirit of her cooking.

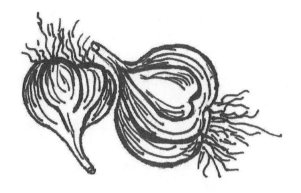

Spaghetti with (Crunchy) Garlic, Oil, and Hot Pepper

This was Papa's favorite, and it became one of mine, once I developed more mature tastes. I am also cheating a bit, doing something different with the garlic. Mama wasn't a fan of garlic. She paid little heed to how it cooked in "Papa's pasta." But when we once made this dish for her, inadvertently turning the garlic brown and crunchy, she thought it was great. So, here is that version.

INGREDIENTS

12 ounces spaghetti

4 tablespoons extra virgin olive oil

4 garlic cloves, cut into small squares, about ⅛ of an inch on each side

1 teaspoon of dried hot red-pepper flakes

Small bunch of Italian parsley, coarsely chopped

Coarse sea salt to taste

PREPARATION

Begin cooking the spaghetti in lightly salted boiling water. When it is almost done, remembering that you want to cook it *al dente*, follow these directions:

In a large skillet, heat the olive oil over high heat until it seems about to smoke. Drop in the garlic and shake quickly, removing the pan from the fire just as the garlic becomes toasted to a light brown color. (This is tricky; timing is important. If the oil is allowed to get too hot, it will begin to burn. So will the garlic if it remains cooking too long. With an electric stove, the coil remains hot after the heat is turned down or off; therefore, at the right moment, the pan must be moved off the unit, and then back again as the cooking proceeds.)

Set the heat at medium and add the pepper flakes and a sprinkle of coarse sea salt. Just before draining the spaghetti, add the parsley. Add the drained spaghetti to the oil/garlic/pepper pan and mix vigorously, seeing to it that all the strands are coated.

Serves 4

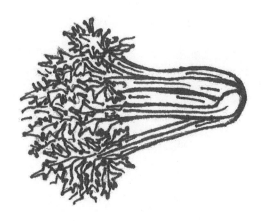

Fresh Pasta with Celery Leaves, Prosciutto, and Tomato

This is an unusual pasta dish that Mama devised. She didn't make it often, but it was one of my favorites. It may take some looking to find a market that doesn't cut off and discard celery leaves before selling the stalks. Once obtained, the leaves are included in the dish with care. Covering them in too much of the tomatoes mutes their distinctive flavor. Conversely, using too many leaves makes the flavor too strong for some people. When everything comes together, this unique dish has a fresh flavor evocative of springtime.

INGREDIENTS

3–4 ounces prosciutto, cut or broken into ½-inch pieces (see below)

4 tablespoons olive oil

1½ cups tomatoes, either in purée form or peeled, seeded and cut in strips

A pinch of salt

1 cup celery leaves, roughly torn

1 clove garlic, minced

¼ teaspoon hot red-pepper flakes

12 ounces fresh homemade pasta sheets or store-bought fresh lasagne sheets, cut into pieces 1 inch wide by 2½ inches long

Grated Parmigiano Reggiano to taste (optional)

PREPARATION

Mama sautéd the prosciutto with some of the other ingredients. I prefer the prosciutto prepared as Giada De Laurentiis demonstrated on a Cooking Channel segment: the prosciutto is laid out on aluminum foil, the pieces not touching, and placed on a cookie sheet. The strips are baked at 350 degrees until they are crispy, about 16–18 minutes. Then they are cut or broken into pieces.

While the prosciutto is in the oven, take the following steps:

In a small saucepan, over medium-high heat, cook the tomatoes in 1½ tablespoons of the oil. Add the salt. If the tomatoes are cut in strips, stir until they become soft and most of the water from them evaporates.

Place the remaining oil in a separate, larger pan and sauté the celery leaves, garlic, and hot red-pepper flakes over medium-high heat. Sauté only for a minute or so, just until all the leaves are tender and coated with the oil.

Pour the tomatoes into the saucepan with the leaves, add the prosciutto pieces when they are done, and mix well. Meanwhile, cook the pasta in boiling, slightly salted water. This should take just a few minutes. Drain the pasta, place it in the large saucepan, and stir well over medium heat.

Serve with the grated Parmigiano Reggiano if desired. (Note: If you prefer the prosciutto to be crispier, sprinkle it on the pasta just before serving.)

Serves 4

Pasta and Lentils

Ah, this dish—I remember it well. I liked it, of course, but, also, it was my job to pick the stones out of the heap of dried lentils that Mama would set out on the table in front of me. In those faraway days, there were more stones among the little flying-saucer-shaped lentils than now. I guess this is due to more efficient harvesting techniques in recent years. When I cooked lentils recently, I found only one stone in a cup and a half of green lentils.

Athough I clearly remember picking out stones and eating the finished product, I never watched Mama as she put this dish together. And this was not one of the dishes she was videotaped making in her ninetieth year.

After some recipe-reading and experimentation, however, I came up with a very reasonable copy of Mama's pasta and lentils, a specialty of her native Italian region of Campania, and a healthful one—a good source of cholesterol-lowering fiber, protein, and iron. I have added one ingredient Mama wouldn't have used, though: crunchy pancetta, Italian cured (not smoked) bacon.

INGREDIENTS

3 cups chicken stock

1 cup green or brown lentils, picked over for stones and rinsed in cold water

3 tablespoons extra virgin olive oil, plus some extra for finishing the dish

½ cup pancetta, cut into small cubes, rind and most fat removed

½ cup diced celery stalks, strings removed

2 cloves garlic

½ small sweet onion, diced

3 large Roma tomatoes, peeled, seeded, and sliced lengthwise into thin strips

½ teaspoon sea salt

½ teaspoon hot red-pepper flakes

1 tablespoon chopped parsley

8 ounces small-cut pasta, such as ditalini

Grated Parmigiano Reggiano (optional)

PREPARATION

Bring the chicken stock to a boil in a saucepan. Add the lentils. Lower the heat and simmer until the lentils are tender, about 35 minutes. Stir occasionally and add stock if the lentils become too dry. However, they should not be soupy.

In a skillet, sauté the pancetta in a tablespoon of oil over medium-low heat, until the fat is rendered and the meat turns slightly brown, about 6 minutes. Remove the pancetta to a paper towel and pat it dry.

After taking out the pancetta, wipe the skillet clean of the oil and fat. Add two tablespoons of oil and cook the celery over medium-low heat, until it begins to soften. Add the garlic and the onion, and continue cooking until the onion becomes soft.

Add the tomatoes, a half-teaspoon of sea salt, and the hot-pepper flakes. Continue cooking until the tomatoes are very soft. Add the pancetta and the lentils. Mix well, adding a little oil if the mixture seems too dry. Discard the garlic cloves.

Cook 8 ounces of the pasta in slightly salted water until it is *al dente*, reserving one-half to one cup of the pasta water.

Drain the pasta and add it and the parsley to the lentil mixture. Continue cooking as you toss everything well, adding the pasta water, as needed, to maintain moisture. Drizzle olive oil over each dish as it is served. Parmigiano Reggiano may be added, as well, if you like. Another idea: substitute rice for the pasta.

Serves 4

Pasta and Ceci from Scratch

This dish can be made quite well and simply with store-bought pasta and canned ceci (chickpeas or garbanzo beans). It becomes a whole other experience when you start with the dried beans and make your own pasta; the work pays off with a tastier and more nutritious dish, not to mention a feeling of satisfaction for having created it from scratch. Mama made it both ways. It was a great winter starter, though welcome in any season. Here's the homemade version:

INGREDIENTS

For the beans:

1 cup dried ceci

2½ tablespoons extra virgin olive oil, plus a little for drizzling at the end

2 large cloves garlic

1 large tomato, skinned, seeded, and cut into thin strips

1 teaspoon Italian aromatic herbs (packaged versions can include some combination of rosemary, sage, thyme, marjoram, onion powder, and oregano, or, you can mix them yourself)

¼ teaspoon oregano, if not in the mixed herbs

Kosher salt and freshly ground black pepper

Grated Parmigiano Reggiano cheese

For the pasta:

1 cup all-purpose flour

1 cup semolina flour

Salt

2 whole eggs, plus an egg yolk

1 tablespoon olive oil

PREPARATION

Place the ceci in a pot with 4 cups of water and soak overnight, covered. Change the water and bring it to a boil. Reduce the heat and simmer the beans for two hours. Taste for tenderness and simmer a few minutes longer, if needed. In the cooking, the ceci double in volume.

In the meantime, make the pasta:

Sift the flour, both all-purpose and semolina, along with a pinch of salt. Make a mound of the flour and fashion a hole in the middle of it. Place the eggs, lightly beaten, in the hole, along with the olive oil, and mix well with the flour.

Knead the flour and egg vigorously and for as long as it takes to create a smooth, cohesive ball. Sprinkle flour over the work generously to minimize the wet mass sticking to hands and cutting board or countertop surface.

When the ball is ready, wrap it tightly in plastic and let it sit for at least 30 minutes. Then cut the ball into quarters. Working with one quarter at a time, spread out the dough with a rolling pin (or run it through a pasta machine) until it is as thin as you can make it. Cut the rolled-out dough in strips lengthwise and across, into 1-inch by 1-inch pieces. Sprinkle them with semolina or regular flour and let them rest on a clean cloth.

In a large pan, heat 2½ tablespoons of oil and sauté the garlic in it. Add the tomato and cook it until it softens. Drain the ceci and add to the pan, putting aside a half cup. Put the reserved ceci in a blender or food processor and purée, adding a little water along the way.

Add the puréed ceci to the whole ones and the tomato in the large pan. Sprinkle on the herbs, some salt and black pepper to taste. Discard the garlic. Mix all ingredients well and keep them warm.

Cook the pasta in boiling water until it is *al dente*, reserving a cup of the pasta water. Drain the pasta and add it to the ceci and tomato, bringing up the heat and tossing everything well. Add the pasta water a little at a time as the contents of the pan thicken. The pasta and ceci should be neither too dense nor too watery.

Serve each portion of the pasta and ceci drizzled with a little olive oil and freshly ground Parmigiano Reggiano.

Serves 4–6

Fresh Cavatelli and Broccoli Rabe

The traditional broccoli-rabe-and-pasta dish is made with store-bought orechiette—pasta shaped like little ears. That's fine. Mama's version was more distinctive with the substitution of cavatelli—short, torpedo-like pasta with a slight curl—that she made herself. It takes more time, but there is something about the combination of the plain-tasting chewy pasta and the bitter greens that make this dish special.

INGREDIENTS

2 cups all-purpose flour

¼ cup or less water

2 bunches broccoli rabe (rapini)

3 tablespoons olive oil

1 garlic clove, chopped

1 teaspoon hot red-pepper flakes

Salt to taste

Juice from half a lemon

Grated Parmigiano Reggiano to taste

MAKING THE PASTA

Lay out the flour in a mound on a board. Make a hole in the center and drip in water, a tablespoon at a time, mixing it with the flour. Knead the dough continuously, adding a bit of water as needed. Not too much water. The dough should be firm.

Keep kneading, forcefully, with the heels of the hands. Every so often, turn the dough in on itself. At other times, break off chunks and then fold them back into the dough ball. When the dough feels smooth yet firm, after 10 minutes or more of kneading, break it into four equal balls. Flour them, put them in a deep dish, cover them with another dish, and set them aside for at least an hour.

Spreading more flour, knead each ball again briefly. With a rolling pin, extend each into an eight-inch circle. With a sharp knife or pizza cutter, slice the dough into strips a half-inch wide. Line up the strips four abreast and cut them into half-inch squares. Roll each square into a little ball and then into an oblong shape. Curl up the sides into the shape of a little boat. (You can use the thin edge of a spoon handle.)

Lay the cavatelli out on a clean cotton or linen cloth, sprinkle lightly with flour, and let sit for a couple hours.

BUILDING THE DISH

Wash the broccoli rabe. Discard the tough stems and separate the leaves from the florets. In a pasta pot of boiling, salted water, cook the florets and leaves for no more than two minutes. Drain the broccoli rabe and set it aside, reserving all the water.

Bring that water to a boil again and cook the cavatelli in it until the pasta all rises to the top and is cooked through but firm.

While the pasta is cooking, heat the oil in a large saucepan or sauté pan. Sauté the garlic and hot red-pepper flakes over medium-high heat. Add the broccoli rabe and sauté for a minute or two. Add a pinch of salt. Drain the pasta well and add it to the pan, mixing all the ingredients together over medium-high heat. Add a little more oil or water, if necessary, and then the lemon juice.

Serve with Parmigiano Reggiano for those who want it.

Serves 4

Fresh Fettucine with Peas and Tomatoes

Here's a dish that features fresh pasta, a vegetable—in this case peas—and tomatoes that have been seeded and peeled. That was Mama's way. I make it with a dash of wine, about which there would have been no need to tell her.

INGREDIENTS

3 tablespoons extra virgin olive oil

¼ small white onion, chopped fine

5 medium plum tomatoes

2 tablespoons dry white wine, or dry white vermouth

1 16-ounce can premium petite peas, ready to heat and serve

Salt and black pepper to taste

¼ teaspoon dried marjoram

¼ teaspoon dried tarragon

4 ounces unsalted butter

12 ounces fresh fettucine (The pasta can be homemade, cut from sheets of the fresh lasagne dough sold in some stores, or the packaged kind found refrigerated in supermarkets.)

Grated Parmigiano Reggiano

PREPARATION

In a large skillet over medium heat, warm the olive oil and sauté the onion until it is translucent.

Boil the tomatoes for about 10 seconds or so, remove the skins and seeds, and cut into quarter-inch strips. Add the tomatoes to the onions and oil, and sauté over medium-high heat until the tomato strips become soft.

Add the wine or vermouth and reduce the liquid by half (the time needed depends on the juiciness of the tomatoes).

Add the peas, some salt and black pepper, the marjoram, and the tarragon. Stir in the butter, in chunks, until melted, and simmer all over low heat.

Cook the pasta in lightly salted water. This usually takes a few minutes. When the pasta is almost ready to be removed from the water, raise the heat under the skillet. Drain the pasta and place it into the skillet, stirring so all the pasta is coated and the peas are evenly distributed.

Turn the pasta and peas onto plates quickly, with Parmigiano Reggiano to taste.

Serves 4

Fresh Pasta with Chard, Beans, and Tomatoes

Here's another pasta dish containing greens and tomatoes, with beans added. Mama made versions of it, close to this hearty combination.

INGREDIENTS

3–4 tablespoons olive oil

2 cloves garlic, chopped fine

¼ teaspoon hot red-pepper flakes

2 large bunches green chard, washed, stalks and thick veins discarded, and leaves roughly torn

2 tablespoons white wine

14-ounce can imported peeled San Marzano tomatoes, chopped, with liquid

14-ounce cannelini beans, drained

½ teaspoon coarse sea salt

Pinch oregano

12 ounces fresh homemade pasta, or store-bought fresh lasagne sheets, in either case cut in pieces about 1 inch wide and 2½ inches long.

PREPARATION

In a large saucepan or sauté pan, sauté the garlic and pepper flakes in 2 tablespoons of the oil over medium-high heat until they sizzle.

Add another tablespoon of the oil and a third of the chard, tossing quickly until the chard is completely coated in the oil and begins to soften slightly. Add another third of the chard and, when coated, add the third handful. The greens should still be crispy.

Add the wine and a bit more olive oil, if needed, and then cook, covered, over medium-low heat for about 6 minutes. Uncover and continue cooking until the liquid is all but evaporated.

Add the tomatoes with their liquid. Add the beans, drained. Add the sea salt and a pinch of oregano.

Continue cooking over medium heat while the pasta boils in lightly salted water. When the pasta is cooked, drain it and mix thoroughly with the contents of the pan. Turn the entire mixture into a large bowl and toss again.

Serve quickly with a sprinkling of Parmigiano Reggiano to taste.

Serves 4

Fresh Pasta with Dandelions, Sausage, and Cherry Tomatoes

This fresh-pasta dish includes some items Mama normally would not have put in pasta—dandelions, grilled sausage, wine, and cherry tomatoes (with skins!)—but the overall effect is comfortably subdued and wholesome.

INGREDIENTS

3 tablespoons olive oil

1 large clove garlic, minced

½ teaspoon hot red-pepper flakes

2 large bunches dandelion greens, washed with stems discarded and leaves roughly torn

½ pound small to medium cherry tomatoes, halved

1 teaspoon coarse sea salt

¼ cup dry white wine

2 large Italian-style sweet sausage links, grilled to well done, cooled, sliced into ¼-inch rounds, and then quartered.

12 ounces fresh pasta (Start with homemade sheets, or fresh store-bought lasagne sheets. Cut into strips roughly 1 inch wide and 2½ inches long. Another option is to use fresh packaged fettucine from the supermarket, cut into 3-inch lengths.)

Grated Parmigiano Reggiano to taste

PREPARATION

In a large sauté pan over medium-high heat, warm 2 tablespoons of the olive oil and sauté the garlic and pepper flakes until the oil sizzles.

Add the dandelion greens and sauté, stirring quickly until tender. Add the cherry tomatoes and salt. Continue sautéing over medium-high heat until the tomato halves are slightly softened.

Add the remaining tablespoon of olive oil, the wine, and the sausage. Simmer until everything is heated through and the liquid is reduced considerably.

Cook the pasta in slightly salted boiling water. It should be done in 2–3 minutes if store-bought, probably longer if homemade. Drain the pasta and stir into the ingredients in the pan. Turn the contents into a large bowl and mix some more. The idea is to get the pasta, dandelions, sausage pieces and tomatoes evenly distributed in the bowl, and then into individual serving portions.

Serve with the grated Parmigiano Reggiano to taste.

Serves 4

A Pasta Dish a la Francaise

Mama would never cook a French dish of any sort, not because of any animosity toward the French, but because she had only a modest knowledge of France and its vaunted cuisine. And she undoubtedly would have found that cuisine a little too rich and slippery for her tastes. This pasta dish, on the other hand, is something she could appreciate. A little rich, yes, but smooth and subtle, with delicate main ingredients.

Then again, this dish is not exactly French. I have labeled it such because of the two main ingredients—one is a product of France and the other sounds as if it should be. The main ingredient is a frilly, divinely light egg pasta, the Valfleuri brand's Pates d'Alsace "lasagnette." I surmise the "little lasagne" name was given because the pasta pieces, though small in size, are rimmed with the curls seen on large, commercially prepared and packaged lasagne sheets.

In truth, any small, light egg pasta would do well in this dish, but probably wouldn't outdo this near-perfect little French creation. It can be found in high-end food stores, even Italian specialty shops secure enough in the quality of their own fare to be unafraid of some competition from Gallic pasta-makers. Balducci's sells me my supply, a part of which goes to my little granddaughter Sarah, who has decided this is her favorite pasta of all time.

The other main ingredient of this dish comes in a can: Le Sueur brand's "Very Young Small Early [or 'Sweet' on some cans] Peas." These peas do not come from France, as the name on the can would have you think, but from Minnesota. It would be nice to make this dish with *fresh* "very young small early" peas, but you'd have to be in an area where they are amply grown, acquire them in season, and then cook them with tender perfection. Believe me—and a host of Le Sueur small-pea aficionados you find when you Google the brand—these tasty little gray-green pearls are just as good, perhaps better.

INGREDIENTS

2 tablespoons olive oil

8 ounces minimally spiced tomato sauce, purée style, homemade or store-bought

8–9 ounces light, small egg pasta, preferably Valfleuri's Pate d'Alsace Lasagnette

1 stick sweet butter

4 ounces heavy cream

Sea salt and freshly ground black pepper

8 ounces Le Sueur brand very young small early peas

⅓ cup shredded basil leaves

Grated Parmigiano Reggiano

PREPARATION

Warm the olive oil in a pan and simmer the tomato sauce.

Cook the pasta in plenty of salted water until *al dente* (okay, in French, *a' la dent*). Just before the pasta is finished, start melting the butter in a large pan over low heat. Drain the pasta and toss it quickly with the butter until all the pasta is coated.

Slowly add the cream, stirring, and then the tomato sauce. Raise the heat to medium. Add a large pinch of sea salt and freshly ground black pepper.

Stir in can of drained Le Sueur baby peas. Keep heating the mixture until the peas are very warm. Add the basil and toss again.

Serve with grated Parmigiano Reggiano passed at the table.

Serves 4 as a first course, 2 as a second

Mentuccia Pasta

Mentuccia, as the name implies, is a member of the very crowded mint family. It's quite a bit shyer than the rest of the flock, at least in America. In Italy, calamintha nepeta, as mentuccia is known formally, can be found more easily, although even there you won't see it mentioned on many menus. That's because it's not a star in its own right, but used to flavor other dishes, including fish and artichokes.

I sought it out in both countries to compare it with the elusive pullia of my parents' ancestral landscape in Italy. (See the separate chapter on pullia at the end of the book.) In Rome, I found some mentuccia at one of our favorite restaurants, and a recipe closely following a dish from that establishment is below. Mentuccia turned out to have a subtler mint taste than my beloved pullia, but was flavorful nonetheless.

Back home, I came across a landscaper in Chicago who sells and ships mentuccia by the potful. I ordered some, and it is flourishing in my side yard. For your information, the mentuccia purveyor can be e-mailed at michael@lapanlandscapes.com.

The restaurant in Rome is Osteria Margutta, on Via Margutta. Its owner, Andrea Tidei, uses mentuccia in the more conventional ways, but also includes it in a light and tasty pasta dish. It goes like this:

INGREDIENTS

3 tablespoons olive oil

¾ pound baby zucchini, scored all around with a fork and cut into ¼-inch-wide rounds

½ teaspoon sea salt and ½ teaspoon freshly ground black pepper

12 ounces short pasta, such as penne or shells

¼ to ½ cup water, reserved from the pasta pot

1 cup mentuccia leaves, torn, with stems removed

1 cup grated sharp Pecorino Romano cheese

PREPARATION

Heat the oil in a broad sauté pan. With the heat medium-high, add the zucchini rounds and cook until soft. Add the sea salt and black pepper to the zucchini and remove from heat.

Cook the pasta in boiling, lightly salted water until *al dente*. Drain and add it to the zucchini. Return the pan to medium-high heat and toss the pasta with the zucchini. Add as much of the reserved water as needed to keep the pasta moist.

Stir in the mentuccia leaves and toss well.

Transfer the contents of the pan to a large bowl. Thoroughly stir in the Pecorino Romano cheese. Serve hot.

Serves 4

Calming Rice and Zucchini Soup

Here's a "stolen" recipe along the lines of one of Mama's dishes. It's a smooth soup of zucchini and rice, found in a cookbook by Antonietta Terrigno of Osteria de Medici Ristorante in Calgary, Alberta, Canada.

I and a number of others in our family fell in love with this soup immediately. I even pronounced it my favorite soup of all time. There is something extremely calming about it. It has simple, wholesome ingredients and no flashy fixings. Mama approved of that.

INGREDIENTS

1 tablespoon butter

3 tablespoons olive oil

1 small onion, chopped fine

1 garlic clove, minced

3 medium-sized zucchini, diced (I cut them crosswise, a quarter-inch thick, and then slice the disks in quarters.)

2 medium to large fresh tomatoes, peeled, seeded, and chopped

8 cups chicken broth

1½ cups long-grain rice, uncooked

Kosher salt and freshly grated black pepper to taste

Grated Parmigiano Reggiano (optional)

PREPARATION

In a large saucepan, heat the butter and oil, and sauté the onion and garlic until both are wilted. Add the zucchini and the tomatoes and mix well.

Simmer for 45 minutes. Add the broth, rice, salt, and pepper, and bring to a boil.

Reduce the heat and simmer until the rice is tender, stirring frequently. As the rice expands, the soup will thicken. It's meant to be served before the liquid becomes fully absorbed in the rice. Add extra broth (or water) if needed to reach the right consistency.

Serve with a sprinkling of Parmigiano Reggiano, if desired.

Serves 4

Capellini with Shrimp and Grape Tomatoes

This recipe and the following one are related. This one uses shrimp and the other adds clams. Both are well-suited to a summer repast.

INGREDIENTS

3 tablespoons extra virgin olive oil

2 large garlic cloves, whole

¼ teaspoon hot red-pepper flakes

8 ounces clam juice

3 pints grape tomatoes, halved lengthwise

1 tablespoon tomato paste

¾ pound medium-size shrimp, heads and tails removed, and shelled and deveined

Sea salt

Basil, roughly torn

12 ounces capellini or other thin imported spaghetti

PREPARATION

Sauté the garlic cloves and pepper flakes in the oil, in a broad pan over medium-high heat. After a minute or two, add the clam juice and bring to a boil. As the mixture begins to evaporate, add the tomatoes. When they begin to shrivel, add the tomato paste, stirring well. Continue thickening the mixture. Add the shrimp and the sea salt to your taste.

As the shrimp just begin turning a light pink, cook the capellini in lightly salted water until *al dente*. This should take about 2 or 3 minutes. In the meantime, the shrimp should have been cooked through and turned a darker pink. Remove the garlic cloves and discard them.

Add the basil to the tomatoes and shrimp, then add the pasta, tossing well.

Serves 4

Capellini with Clams and Shrimp

Somehow, this pasta dish comes off as rich and airy at the same time, a hallmark of many of Mama's offerings. Its aroma is satisfying enough. The combination of flavors more than satisfies the taste buds.

INGREDIENTS

4 tablespoons olive oil

3 garlic cloves, finely chopped

2 tablespoons finely sliced green onion, white and light green parts

½ teaspoon hot red-pepper flakes

½ cup clam juice, and then some

½ cup dry white wine, and then some

Sea salt to taste

16 littleneck or manila clams

½ pound shelled, deveined medium-size shrimp

2 tablespoons Italian parsley, roughly chopped

8 ounces capellini or thin spaghetti

PREPARATION

Sauté the garlic, green onions, and hot pepper in a broad pan with hot oil. When these ingredients are softened, add the clam juice and the wine. Sprinkle with a dash of salt and bring to a boil.

Add the clams, keeping the liquid at a boil.

When the first clam starts to open, add the shrimp. Keep adding clam juice and wine, alternately and a little at a time, as the liquid condenses. As more clams open, add the parsley and continue stirring.

Cook the capellini in lightly salted boiling water, following package directions for making the pasta *al dente*.

When all the clams are open and the shrimp are pink, pour the drained pasta into the pan and stir vigorously. Pour the contents into a large dish and serve.

Serves 4

Lobster-Sauced Spaghetti:
Star of Christmas Eves

For as long as anyone can remember, Christmas Eve dinners in Italian-American households have revolved around fish—all kinds, made in all ways. Mama stuck with the tradition.

There was one standout on the menu: spaghetti with lobster sauce. It was always simply made, and that's why, in my opinion, it was so good—good enough to linger in memory well into the rest of the holiday season. And good enough to make year round.

INGREDIENTS

2 tablespoons extra virgin olive oil

2 cloves garlic, minced

1 teaspoon hot red pepper flakes

20 ounces tomato sauce (see note below)

½ teaspoon sea salt

4 medium-size lobster tails or 8 small ones (3½–4 inches long), rinsed, still in the shell

12 ounces imported spaghetti

2 tablespoons basil, torn coarsely

PREPARATION

In a broad saucepan or skillet, over medium-high heat, warm the oil, garlic and pepper flakes. When the oil starts to sizzle, add the tomato sauce and the salt.

(Note: As for the sauce, Mama used only sauce derived from strained tomatoes, with good effect. No skins, seeds, or chunks. Of course, she used the purée that she and her lady friends put up in jars every fall, which I recounted earlier in the book. The strained tomatoes had nothing added, but got their flavor from the oil, garlic, and hot pepper with which they were infused. If you haven't made your own strained tomatoes, you can use any one of several commercial products imported from Italy. They contain strained tomatoes and nothing else. The bottom line is that this form of smooth sauce is best because it doesn't have chunks competing in taste and texture with the delicate lobster meat.)

Raise the heat under the sauce. When it has bubbled for a minute or two, add the lobster tails, still in their shells. In the meantime, cook the spaghetti in lightly salted boiling water.

Cook the lobster for about 10 minutes, if you've used the larger tails, or about 6 minutes if you've used the smaller ones.

Lift them from the sauce, and when they've cooled slightly, remove the meat from the shells with kitchen shears. Cut the shorn tails into 1½-inch wide pieces and return them to the sauce, along with the basil.

Pour the sauce over the drained pasta, toss well, and serve.

Serves 4

Unlikely Lasagne:
Four Cheeses, Veggies …
and No Tomato Sauce!

Mama made lasagne, and it was great, but I don't think it was significantly different from the lasagne other mamas and grandmas make. Perhaps, Mama gave a little more attention to eliminating gravy fat, if she was using meat sauce; however, I have not included her lasagne here.

Instead, I offer an unusual and very satisfying lasagne. It's not that light (lots of cheese; think of the protein) and not that quick to assemble (so it should be a work for two), but every time we've made this dish, it's been a satisfying and praiseworthy first or main course.

We came upon the recipe by chance on the web. Research showed it had originally appeared in a publication of Reiman Publications, LLC. We adapted the recipe by substituting two ingredients that tended to "Italianize" it, though that was not our intention. We used zucchini rather than broccoli, and ricotta rather than cottage cheese.

INGREDIENTS

2 tablespoons vegetable oil

3 garlic cloves, minced

2 cups chopped zucchini

1½ cups julienned carrots

1 cup thinly sliced green onions

½ cup chopped sweet red pepper

½ cup all-purpose flour

3 cups whole milk

½ cup grated Parmigiano Reggiano, divided

½ teaspoon salt

¼ teaspoon black pepper

1 package (10 ounces) frozen chopped spinach, thawed and drained

1½ cups whole milk ricotta cheese

1 cup shredded mozzarella cheese

½ cup shredded Swiss cheese

12 lasagne noodles, cooked and drained ("no boil" noodles can be used
as well)

PREPARATION

In a skillet, sauté the garlic, zucchini, carrots, onions, and pepper in the
oil until they are crisp but still tender. Place the skillet aside.

In a heavy saucepan, whisk the flour and milk until smooth. Bring this
to a boil; cook and stir for 2 minutes. (Don't let the mixture burn on the
bottom.) Reduce the heat. Add ¼ cup of the grated cheese, the salt, and
the pepper. Cook one minute longer or until the cheese is melted.

Remove the saucepan from the heat and stir in the spinach. Set one
cup of the mixture aside.

In a bowl, combine the ricotta, mozzarella, and Swiss cheeses.

Spread ½ cup of the spinach mixture onto a greased 13-inch by 9-inch by
2-inch baking dish. Make a layer with four noodles, half of the cheese mixture
and vegetables, and ¾ cup of the spinach mixture. Repeat the layers.

Top with the remaining noodles, the reserved spinach mixture, and
the grated cheese. Cover and bake at 375 degrees for 35 minutes. Uncover
and bake 15 minutes longer or until the lasagne is bubbly. Let stand for 15
minutes (preferably longer) before cutting.

(Note: The lasagne noodles should be very thin. You can make them
yourself, with a lot of elbow grease or passes through the pasta machine, or
you can buy commercially available "no boil" noodles; however, the latter
can be thick, so look for the ones that are not.)

Serves 6–8

Old-Fashioned Ravioli

I didn't think of Mama's ravioli as old-fashioned at the time. It was just smooth, unadorned, and tasty. For me, ravioli was among the best pastas that Mama made.

Reflecting now on how she made them, and what went into them, I think the description of "old-fashioned" fits. In the first place, the pasta was created without any ravioli-making tools, with the exception of a wine glass, a fork, and a safety pin. Hers was a rather bizarre process, to be sure, devoid of the use of any appliances.

Second, the filling of the ravioli included none of the fancy fixings one sees these days in trendy food shops and restaurants—anything from squash to pesto to ground veal and pork. Mama's ravioli were filled only with ricotta mixed with an egg, and just a taste of two other cheeses.

I write this after watching Mama make the ravioli as she, at ninety, was videotaped doing so in her bright kitchen. The tape does not show her making the remarkably light pasta she used for these ravioli, however; it only appears in the video as a perfectly smooth ball, ready to be rolled and shaped. After some experimentation, though, I think I've come close to the way Mama made the dough. The descriptions for making the filling and forming the ravioli follow her taped procedures.

INGREDIENTS

For the pasta dough:

1 cup all-purpose flour, sifted

¼ cup semolina, sifted, plus some for spreading on the kneading board

1 egg, lightly beaten

1 tablespoon olive oil

For the filling:

¾ cup whole-milk ricotta

¼ cup loosely packed, shredded mozzarella

1 heaping tablespoon grated Parmigiano Reggiano or pecorino cheese

1 egg

Salt and pepper to taste

PREPARATION

Mix the dough ingredients together carefully by hand, then knead the dough vigorously on a semolina-sprinkled board or tabletop. Keep pressing down with the heel of the hand, and turning the dough in on itself until you have a smooth, firm ball. If the mixture is dry, put some water in the bowl in which the egg had been beaten and add it to the dough a tiny bit at a time as you knead.

Put the dough ball in a dish, cover it with another dish, and let it sit for about three hours.

For the filling, combine the ricotta, the mozzarella, the grated cheese, the egg, and a little salt and pepper. Whip the mixture energetically with a fork until it is very smooth.

Roll out the dough as thinly as possible without tearing it. The consistency should be slightly elastic.

Place three or four dollops of the filling, each about a generous teaspoonful, along one side of the dough. The dollops should be about an inch and a half from the edge of the dough and the same distance apart. Holding the edge of the dough, lift it over the little mounds of filling and press it down. To differentiate the dollops, place the side of one hand on either side of each dollop and press down gently.

Then get a wine glass, or any sturdy glass with a stem, whose opening is ideally 2¾ inches in diameter. A shade more or less wide is okay. Place the glass on top of each dollop, so that the cheese mixture takes up half of the glass's opening. Press down on the stem and twist the glass so it cuts through the dough, creating half-moon-shaped ravioli.

Repeat the folding and cutting procedure until all the dough has been used. (As each line of dollops is made into ravioli, excess pieces of dough form. They can be cut away, rekneaded and rolled out to make a few more ravioli.)

As each of the ravioli is formed, crimp it firmly around the cut edges with a fork. Sprinkle some semolina on a broad cookie sheet and place the ravioli on it. Puncture the ravioli with a safety pin or sewing needle, giving each about a half dozen little jabs.

Cover the ravioli on the cookie sheet with tight-fitting plastic wrap, then aluminum foil, and freeze. As Mama said, the freezing helps insure the ravioli do not open during cooking. The pinpricks are to allow them to vent a little.

When you want to prepare the ravioli, drop them, still frozen, into salted, boiling water. When all have risen to the top, continue a low boil for a minute or so. Test one of the ravioli for doneness, then drain.

For toppings, choose either a simple, smooth tomato sauce or a sauce of butter, a little cream, and fresh sage leaves, with plenty of grated cheese for either version.

Serves up to 4 (16–20 ravioli)

MAIN COURSES

Bistecca Alla Pizzaiola
(Steak in Tomato Sauce)

Here's a dish that is appreciated by those who like steak and don't mind having it served with spicy tomato sauce (as opposed to broiled and bloody), and by those who like spicy tomato sauce and don't mind having it served with steak.

It's an old southern Italian standby—*bistecca*, or steak, *alla pizzaiola*. It was one of the quicker dishes Mama could put together for the family after she got home from work.

INGREDIENTS

2 pounds lean, thin sirloin steaks, including sirloin-tip sandwich steaks, or minute steaks (try thin-cut T-bone steaks)

2 tablespoons extra virgin olive oil

1 clove garlic, chopped

4 Roma tomatoes, skins, seeds, and white membranes removed, cut in ¼-inch strips

1 cup strained tomatoes (purée)

Salt and hot red-pepper flakes to taste

Handful Italian parsley, roughly torn

PREPARATION

Cut away most of the peripheral fat from the steaks. Rub in a little salt.

In a large skillet, sauté the garlic in 1½ tablespoons of the olive oil until the oil begins to sizzle. Add the cut tomatoes and bring them to a quick boil. Add the strained tomatoes, a little salt, and a pinch of hot-pepper flakes. Reduce the heat and let the tomatoes simmer.

Use a separate skillet for the steaks. (Cooking them in the same pan as the tomatoes means any fat in them gets mixed in with everything else. Not to Mama's taste.) Over very high heat, spread a small amount of oil in the skillet. Cook the steaks quickly, just until they brown on both sides, and not too long or they will become tough. Pat them to remove excess moisture and transfer them to the skillet with the tomatoes.

Spoon the tomatoes over the steaks and add the parsley. Cover and cook over medium-low heat for about 5 minutes. (You can put little knife cuts on the corners of the steaks to prevent them from curling.)

Serves 4

Savory Chicken Breasts

Here's a tasty, relatively easy-to-make, wholesome, and colorful chicken dish, as good the day after as it is freshly cooked. The hardest part may be preparing the chicken in a method favored by Mama.

INGREDIENTS

1½ to 2 pounds chicken breasts, sliced and/or pounded thin

2 tablespoons extra virgin olive oil

1 garlic clove

½ red sweet bell pepper, cut lengthwise into ⅛-inch slices

½ yellow sweet bell pepper, cut the same way

4 large Roma tomatoes, skinned, seeded, and cut lengthwise into ¼-inch slices

½ cup pitted kalamata olives, drained and rinsed

¼ cup bottled capers, drained and rinsed

¼ cup dry white wine or dry vermouth

¼ teaspoon sea salt

Freshly ground black pepper

1 tablespoon Italian parsley, chopped

PREPARATION

With a sharp knife, cut away from the chicken breast slices all visible yellow fat, as well as any white membrane extending into the meat. This will alter the shape of some of the chicken slices, but it will improve their taste, inasmuch as the unappetizing fat and tendons will have been discarded. Rinse the meat, pat it dry, and set it aside.

Preheat the oven to 350 degrees.

Place the oil in a large sauté pan and, over low heat, sauté the garlic clove. Add the peppers and sauté until they soften but do not wilt altogether, 10 to 12 minutes. Remove the peppers and most of the oil from the pan and set aside in a bowl. Discard the garlic clove. Add the cut tomatoes to the peppers and stir.

In the remaining oil, in the same pan, cook the chicken pieces over high heat until they are well-browned on both sides, about 4 minutes total.

Place half of the pepper and tomato mixture in a 9-inch-square glass baking dish. Spread the chicken pieces on top, followed by the olives and capers and, finally, the rest of the peppers and tomatoes.

Bake for 35 minutes. Extract the dish momentarily to add the wine or vermouth, the sea salt, and the black pepper, and return it to the oven for 10 more minutes.

Remove the dish, sprinkle with parsley, cover with foil, and let sit for at least 15 minutes before serving.

Serves 4

Mama's Elusive Vinegar Chicken

This, everyone in the family agrees, was one of Mama's most unusual and noteworthy offerings. As a young girl in Italy, Mama learned to cook vinegar chicken from her big sister Rosaria, which makes the dish about a century old, at least.

It sounds deceptively simple: cut a chicken into small pieces, remove all skin and fat, and fry in olive oil with seasoning—and a lot of vinegar—until well done. In truth, however, it takes attention to detail to produce a reasonable facsimile of Mama's vinegar chicken.

INGREDIENTS

1 small frying chicken, 3 or 4 pounds

3 tablespoons or more olive oil

1 large clove garlic, chopped

Coarse sea salt and black pepper to taste

2 large bay leaves

1 cup or more red wine vinegar, and a little water

PREPARATION

Cut the chicken into 10 to 12 small parts, on the bone. Many supermarkets sell chickens already cut into 8 pieces, giving you less cutting to do. Or, you can do all the cutting yourself from scratch. Try this website link for illustrated directions on chicken-cutting: http://www.gourmetsleuth.com/cutupchicken.htm. A word of caution: as you cut the full breast into a few smaller pieces, take care to remove any small, thin bones attached to the meat.

Once you have the chicken cut up, carefully remove all the skin. The small, outer part of the wings is resistant to skin-removal. If you can't live without the wings, include them as-is in the cooking. Otherwise discard them. Once the skin is off the rest of the bird, use sharp kitchen scissors to remove every spot of yellow fat you can on each piece. Dig into crevices with the point of the scissors to get at hard-to-find deposits. This chicken dish should be as greaseless as possible.

With the chicken's skin and fat gone, Mama would soak the parts in cold, salted water for a short time. My way is to make a proper brine (see below) and soak the chicken in it at length. This moisturizes the bird for the hot frying that lies ahead.

To brine, put the chicken in a large pot containing three quarts of water (or enough to cover), a quarter cup of kosher salt, and two tablespoons of sugar. Cover the pot and refrigerate it for about two hours. (Roughly the directions for brining found in the useful *Cook's Illustrated* magazine.)

Then wash the chicken well under cold running water and set it aside to drain, patting off much of the moisture with paper towels.

Heat three tablespoons of olive oil in a large skillet until simmering. Arrange the chicken parts in the skillet, the oil sizzling as you do so. With a fork or tongs, turn the chicken as it starts to brown, moving the pieces occasionally so they don't stick.

When there is a light brown color on both sides of the pieces, spread the garlic, a teaspoon of sea salt, and black pepper from a few turns of the pepper mill over the chicken. Then drop in the bay leaves. (Mama crumbled the bay leaves as she added them, and left them in the finished dish. To my knowledge, no one ever got a sliver caught in the teeth or lower regions, but I prefer the accepted method of removing bay leaves whole from the cooked food.)

The rest of the cooking consists of adding a bit of water or oil, and generous doses of vinegar over the chicken as it browns. As you notice the evaporating liquid start to dry out the skillet under the chicken, add more liquid—especially the vinegar. Don't skimp on it. Keep the heat high until the browning becomes dark, and then turn the heat to medium and cover the skillet. Add vinegar from time to time.

Most of the pieces will be done, with very dark browning, in about 40 minutes. Check with a meat thermometer if you want to be sure (160 degrees Farenheit is considered done). Remove the breast parts in about 30 minutes.

Discard the bay leaves, give a final generous dousing of vinegar, and remove the chicken to a platter, covering it with foil until it's ready to be served. Eat with the fingers.

Serves 4

Vinegar Steak

Here's another of Mama's unusual meat dishes with vinegar: broiled steak. We did not have an outdoor grill when we lived in Newark, so steaks and chops were cooked under the broiler, filling the house with a mouth-watering aroma. There are numerous steak and London broil recipes that include vinegar in a marinade. This one applies it directly to the meat.

INGREDIENTS

1–1½ pound sirloin steak, about an inch thick, excess fat removed

1 garlic clove (if desired; Mama didn't)

Sea salt

Freshly ground black pepper

¼ cup red wine vinegar, plus a tablespoon

PREPARATION

Set the broiler to high. Rub the steak thoroughly on both sides with the garlic clove, the salt, and the pepper.

Place the steak on a lower rack, 8 to 10 inches from the broiler element, and cook for three minutes per side. Move the steak to an upper rack about 4 inches from the heat and cook for another three minutes per side, for medium doneness. (Mama didn't use this two-rack trick, picked up from Alton Brown on the Food Channel.) With three minutes to go on the final side, pour the vinegar over the steak.

Remove the steak from the oven and let it sit under foil for three to five minutes. Before serving, pour the remaining tablespoon of vinegar over it. Slice the steak thinly across the grain.

Serves 3–4

Braciole (A Beef Rollup),
Minimalist Version

This is not really a recipe. It's a suggestion. Most Italian families are accustomed to a Sunday lunch or dinner favorite: ragú made with meat. The meat is usually sausage, lamb, veal, and beef, the last in the form of braciole, also called involtini, which is rolled up flank or top round.

The preparation for braciole is quite standard and there is no need to go over it much here. The meat is well-browned, then steeped in the cook's favorite tomato sauce for a long, long time. Before browning, the beef is pounded until thin, certain ingredients are placed on it, and it is rolled up and kept secure with toothpicks or cooking string.

The "filling" for the braciole is the subject here: too many cooks put too many things into it for my—and Mama's—minimalist tastes. A perusal of recipes for braciole yielded the following partial list of ingredients to be added in some combination to the filling in the rolled up beef: anchovy paste, boiled eggs, bell pepper, broccoli, currants, croutons, cheese (Parmigiano, provolone, or Locatelli), garlic, kale, mushrooms, onions, pancetta, parsley, pine nuts, prosciutto, and salami.

No doubt, with some combinations of these ingredients, the braciole would be tasty. But I prefer Mama's simple formula for the stuffing, using just two of the above ingredients—garlic and parsley, both minced (along with a touch of salt). You can use as much or little of each as you like. Mama used very little, but the taste that the garlic and parsley imparted to the braciole seemed just right. Above all, it didn't overwhelm or mask the flavor of the beef.

And it's a lasting combination. I prepared the above version of braciole (all fat and gristle removed, of course) and froze some of it in its own tomato sauce. Defrosted and warmed after a long hibernation, it was delicious, just as I remembered the delicacy on Mama's table.

Slow-Cooked Pork Chops

Mama never owned a crock pot, but she occasionally slow-cooked things, like beef and chicken, until they fell apart with the touch of a fork. My wife, Chris, who does own a crock pot, made this analogous dish with pork. These slow-cooked chops are simple, low-fat, conservatively seasoned, and yet flavorful. And they fall apart with the touch of a fork. The recipe is good for two people.

INGREDIENTS

3 tablespoons olive oil

1 large sweet white onion, sliced into thick rings

2 boneless center-cut pork chops, 6-8 ounces each and about ½ to 1 inch thick

1 cup chicken broth

¾ cup dry white wine

Salt and freshly ground black pepper to taste

PREPARATION

In a heavy skillet, sauté the onion rings in the olive oil over medium heat, turning them once. When they are lightly browned on both sides, remove them from the pan and place on a plate.

Using the same pan, turn the heat to medium-high and cook the pork chops until browned, about 2 minutes per side. Remove the chops, as well. Turn the heat off and loosen the trimmings left in the bottom of the pan with a scraper.

Add the chicken broth and wine, and some salt and pepper.

Place the pork chops in the crock pot, with half the onion slices on the bottom and half on top of each chop. Pour the liquid over the chops and onions, and turn on the power to the pot.

Cook 4 to 5 hours on high, or 7 hours on low. Baste the chops once, halfway through the cooking. When the chops are done, transfer them to warmed plates and pour the remaining liquid over them. Serve immediately.

Serves 2

Veal Scaloppini with Green Peppers

There are lots of ways to prepare veal scaloppini, and I like all of them. But Mama's way is still my favorite. It isn't the way you are likely to find them on a menu, where they are usually presented with lemon sauce, marsala, butter, or mushrooms. Her way yielded results more akin to the Milanese veal cutlet, *costolette alla Milanese*, which is breaded and fried. Unlike the Milanese version, however, which can be rather board-like, Mama's scaloppini were not clothed in breadcrumbs, but rather in a thin coating of flour and beaten egg.

The veal was soft and light when sautéed and, best of all, from my perspective, was most accommodating with respect to when you wanted to eat it. Other scaloppini have to be consumed when they are cooked. Mama's, with their protective soft crust, could be made early in the day and eaten at dinnertime. Or, they could be refrigerated, warmed a little, and eaten the next day in a sandwich with peppers—my favorite way.

We often had Mama's scaloppini at supper. But what I preferred was a next-day option, putting them into a hard roll (such as a kaiser roll), with the lemon juice, sautéed peppers, and, if I was feeling cheese-deprived, a little shaved Parmigiano Reggiano atop the veal. Memories linger of Sundays, in the 1940s, on the summery beaches of Long Branch, New Jersey, where Mama dished out tasty sandwiches like this from her floppy day-trip bag.

INGREDIENTS

5 tablespoons olive oil

1 clove garlic, whole

1 large green pepper, cored and cut into ¼-inch strips, lengthwise

Salt and pepper to taste

1½ pounds veal scaloppini, pounded thin between sheets of wax paper

Flour for dredging

2 beaten eggs

2 lemons

PREPARATION

Heat 2 tablespoons of the oil in a skillet, with the clove of garlic. Add the peppers and sauté over medium-high heat for 3 to 5 minutes. Lower the heat, cover, and let the peppers cook until soft, about 10 minutes more. Let them sit, covered. Discard the garlic.

Sprinkle a small of amount of salt and pepper on each piece of veal. Coat each piece thoroughly in the flour, shaking off any excess. Then dip the veal into the beaten egg, making sure it is well-coated.

In a separate large skillet, heat the remaining 3 tablespoons of oil over medium-high heat. When the oil begins to shimmer, add the veal and sauté until it is cooked through and there is a thin, light-brown crust on the meat. If the scaloppini are thin, this should take about 2½ minutes per side. If the veal cannot all fit in one skillet, use another, or clean off the skillet you have and start again with fresh oil. Remove the veal, place on paper towels, and pat away excess oil.

Squeeze the lemons liberally over the veal and serve alongside the peppers.

Serves 4

Veal Spezzatino:
A Stew, Largely Unadorned

By unadorned, I mean lacking ingredients traditionally found in stews—potatoes, onions, mushrooms, other vegetables, even pasta. Of course they could be included in this "spezzatino" (meaning stew, from the Italian word for breaking something into pieces) but it wouldn't be the dish that Mama served and other devotees of simple yet hearty Italian dishes favor. This one highlights just one thing—bite-sized pieces of the tenderest veal imaginable. Mama would also put a vegetable or two on the table next to the spezzatino, just not in it.

The dish is not especially difficult to make. It does take a little patience, because the veal must cook for a long time. To start with, however, a very sharp knife is needed.

INGREDIENTS

1½–2 pounds boneless veal (see PREPARATION section regarding cut)

2 tablespoons olive oil

2 cloves garlic, chopped

⅓ cup white wine

½ cup beef broth

Bay leaf

1 generous teaspoon dried, crushed rosemary

Sea salt and freshly ground black pepper to taste

8 ounces tomato purée, homemade or store-bought (imported)

1½ tablespoons heavy cream at room temperature

2 tablespoons chopped Italian parsley

PREPARATION

One characteristic of Mama's spezzatino was the size and condition of the cubes of veal that formed the heart of the dish. They were small. And they were made as devoid of fat or gristle as possible. A lot of recipes for spezzatino call for 2-inch cubes. Let's make that 1-inch cubes to start with. Unless you have a heaven-sent butcher, when you ask for veal to use in stew, you'll get cubes—most likely the 2- or even 3-inch ones—with a fair amount of flappy white matter attached. Thus, the sharp knife. Cut and prune away the fat or gristle, until you get small cubes of pure pink meat. Be prepared to jettison some pieces that are just too ornery to deal with.

Heat the olive oil over high heat in a large skillet. Brown the veal well on all sides. Add the garlic and wine and, stirring occasionally, allow the liquid to nearly evaporate.

Add the beef broth, bay leaf, rosemary, sea salt, black pepper, and tomato sauce. Bring these to a boil for about two minutes, and then lower the heat to simmer range.

Cover and cook for at least 60 minutes. Stir the stew occasionally and add a little broth or water if it looks too dry. Taste a piece at the 60-minute mark and, if not tender enough, continue cooking for 10 more minutes or so.

About 5 minutes from the end of the cooking, add the heavy cream, slowly, and stir well. The dish should look pinkish. Discard the bay leaf, stir in the parsley, and serve hot.

Serves 4–5

Feather-Light Fried Fish

This was one of the most common fish dishes Mama made when we were growing up. It really was the seafood version of the veal cutlet dish earlier described: the preparation is almost identical. Despite being fried, the fish is nongreasy and very light. And quick to prepare.

INGREDIENTS

5 tablespoons olive oil

Flour for dredging

2 well-beaten eggs

Salt and freshly ground black pepper to taste

4 fillets of sole, flounder, or similarly flaky fish, each fillet about 6 ounces

2 lemons

PREPARATION

Heat half the oil in a large skillet over medium-high heat. Have the flour and the beaten eggs ready in separate dishes, each sprinkled with a little salt and black pepper.

Remove excess moisture from the fillets with a paper towel. Place a pinch of salt and pepper on two of the fillets. Dip them into the flour first. The flouring should cover the entire piece of fish.

Dip the floured fillets into the egg, making sure that all areas are covered. Let excess egg mixture drip off. When a tiny drop of the egg mixture sizzles in the oil, place two fillets in the skillet.

Cook over medium heat, covered, for three or four minutes per side, depending on the thickness of the fillets. The coating should be thin and golden or light brown, and the fish itself white, moist, and flaky.

Remove the fillets from the skillet and place them on thickly folded paper towels. Towel-dry the tops of the fillets, as well, and cover them with foil to keep them warm.

Quickly wipe the skillet clean or use another one. Put in the remaining 2½ tablespoons of oil and repeat the process with the two remaining fillets. (If the skillet is large enough to accommodate all four fillets, fine; otherwise each batch of two should be cooked separately in clean oil.)

Squeeze half a lemon over each fillet. Serve with green beans, dressed with olive oil, lemon, and salt, and mashed or baked potatoes. (Note: Some may wish to eat these fillets with tartar sauce. Unaccustomed to such cloudy condiments, Mama's eyes would grow skeptically wide at the prospect, but be my guest.)

Serves 4

Halibut Steaks with Grape Tomatoes and Capers

Here's another fish recipe that's easy to make and very flavorful.

INGREDIENTS

1 tablespoon olive oil, plus some for drizzling

2 halibut skinless fillets, each about 6 to 8 ounces.

2 lemons

1 tablespoon white wine

Sea salt and freshly ground black pepper

12–15 grape tomatoes, halved

1 tablespoon capers, rinsed

1 tablespoon Italian parsley, chopped

PREPARATION

Preheat the oven to 350 degrees. In a skillet that can later go in the oven, heat 1 tablespoon of oil over high heat. Add the halibut and sear both sides of each piece until they are browned slightly, about 2 minutes a side.

Remove the skillet from the top of the stove, squeeze the juice of one lemon and the tablespoon of wine over the fillets, and place the skillet in the oven.

Bake until the fish just begins to flake, about 10 to 12 minutes. Remove the fillets from the oven, and sprinkle with a small amount of sea salt and the pepper. Reset the oven to 375 degrees. Place the grape tomato halves and capers around and on the fish fillets, then return them to the oven for 2 to 3 minutes, wilting the tomatoes. If the fish looks like it might become too dry, pour another tablespoon of wine or water over it before putting it back in the oven.

Remove the skillet from the oven, squeeze the juice of the other lemon over the fillets, and drizzle a small amount of oil, about a teaspoon, over them. Sprinkle the dish with the parsley and serve hot.

Serves 2

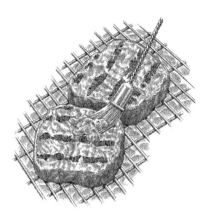

Tuna Steaks with Red and Green Peppers

This is an Italianized version of the trendy tuna dishes favored by many restaurants, whose cooks tend to sear the outside of the tuna and leave the inside blood-colored. You can have this version with the fish as rare as that if you like. Or, as our household does, you can have the tuna a little more on the medium side. You can also use this recipe with swordfish instead of tuna.

INGREDIENTS

4 six-ounce yellowfin tuna steaks

3½ tablespoons extra virgin olive oil

Two large garlic cloves, whole

2 small, sweet bell peppers, 1 red and 1 green, seeded and cut into ¼-inch strips, lengthwise

Marinade:

2 tablespoons olive oil

¼ cup fresh lemon juice

1 cup dry white wine

¼ cup soy sauce

1 tablespoon crushed dry rosemary

1 teaspoon sea salt

1 teaspoon freshly grated black pepper

PREPARATION

Marinate the tuna steaks for between a half-hour and an hour, in a covered casserole dish or plastic bag. If you use the dish, turn the steaks over once or twice, spooning the liquid over them.

Heat the oil and garlic in a skillet over medium-high heat. Add the pepper strips. Lower the heat and stir occasionally, until the peppers soften. Set the skillet aside.

Remove the tuna steaks from the marinade and pat them gently with a paper towel. Place them on a very hot charcoal or gas grill—just long enough for sear marks to appear on both sides.

Transfer the steaks to the skillet containing the oil and peppers. Raise the heat to medium-high and sauté the steaks, with the peppers, for 2 or 3 minutes a side, depending on the level of doneness desired. Taste a pepper strip and add a pinch of salt if desired. Discard the garlic and serve the steaks hot, placed over the peppers.

Serves 4

Brown-Bagging It: Fish in Cartoccio

Flaky fish and fresh vegetables, steamed in their own juices inside a paper bag (cartoccio) or parchment paper; it's hard to imagine a more satisfying main course. The dish exudes a sense of wholesomeness in content, authenticity in flavor, and simplicity in composition—all hallmarks of Mama's kitchen. This recipe is for one serving. Repeat it as many times as there are diners.

INGREDIENTS

Juice of one lemon

1 tablespoon clam juice

1 tablespoon extra virgin olive oil

2 tablespoons dry white wine

¼ cup white or red potatoes, cut into ¾-inch wedges and boiled briefly until slightly cooked

¼ cup zucchini, cut into ¾-inch wedges

¼ cup shitake mushrooms, thinly sliced

Kosher salt and freshly ground black pepper to taste

A 6-ounce fillet of a white, flaky fish such as halibut or cod, about one inch thick

½ teaspoon fresh dill or ¼ teaspoon dried

1 small to medium tomato, skinned, seeded, and thinly sliced lengthwise

4 kalamata olives, pitted, rinsed, and thinly sliced

1 tablespoon capers, rinsed

1 tablespoon fresh parsley, chopped

PREPARATION

Preheat the oven to 400 degrees. Stir together the lemon juice, clam juice, olive oil, and wine, and set aside.

In the center of a 15-inch by 13-inch piece of parchment paper or aluminum foil, make a mound with the potatoes, zucchini, and mushrooms. Sprinkle with a little kosher salt and pepper.

Place the fish on top of the vegetables and sprinkle it with dill and a touch of the salt and pepper. Then top the fish with the tomato, olives, capers, and parsley.

Lift the parchment paper up slightly on all four sides and pour in the liquid. Fold the paper together tightly across the top and on the sides.

Place the bag on a baking sheet and bake for 30 minutes. Carefully open the folded parchment paper. The fish should be moist and flaky, and the vegetables cooked but not mushy. Spoon the liquid over the fish. The contents can be removed and served on a dish, or served in the open bag.

Simple Fish Fillets, Marinated and Baked

Mama didn't go in much for marinating, but this version of fish fillets, steeped first in a marinade with all natural ingredients and then baked, was a hit. Sister Alba makes this dish to perfection. The recipe comes from Rhodesbread.com.

INGREDIENTS

¼ cup fresh lemon juice

¼ cup extra virgin olive oil

1 tablespoon chopped fresh dill or ½ tablespoon dried dill

1 tablespoon Dijon mustard

1 clove garlic, minced

Salt and pepper to taste

1½ pounds fish fillets (anything ranging from tuna or swordfish to halibut, turbot, tilapia, or flounder)

PREPARATION

Set the oven at 375 degrees. Whisk together the lemon juice, olive oil, dill, mustard, garlic, and some salt and pepper. Place the fillets in a baking dish, cover with the mixture, and let stand for an hour.

Remove the fillets from the marinade and place on a flat, ungreased baking pan. Spoon a bit of the marinade over the fillets. Cover lightly with foil and bake them for 10 to 13 minutes, depending on the thickness of the fish. Remove the foil and finish the fillets under the broiler for a minute or two.

Serves 4

Baccalà (Dried Cod) Poached in Herbs and Wine

Growing up, I was not a fan of fish. Mama's fried flounder was all right, though I had difficulty appreciating the fragrance and tried to stay out of the kitchen while it was being cooked. And shrimp, being unfishlike, was all right. But more often than not, while everybody else was eating fish, I would have a scrambled egg—and that was true even during the big Christmas Eve fish feasts. One of Papa's favorite dishes—baccalà, or dried cod fish—I found especially suspect.

My aversion to fish began to crumble when, in my midtwenties, I was sent to live and work in Italy. There I began trying plainly grilled sea bass and other "nonfishy" fishes plucked fresh from the Tyrrhenian Sea. After a couple of years in Italy, I was transferred to Portugal. It was during my year there that I became not only tolerant of fish, but a lover of it. (One of my favorite dishes was sole broiled with banana; another was tiny shrimp baked with garlic, oil, and hot pepper.)

The national food of Portugal is baccalà—*bacalao* in Portuguese. Portugal was a nation of explorers but also of less glamorous but storied fishermen who spent months catching cod in the cold North Atlantic. The cod was dried and salted for the long voyage home. The Portuguese prided themselves on preparing bacalao "101 ways," many versions of which I found quite tasty.

I have memories visiting local fish markets with Mama in Newark when I was a boy. There, hanging on wall hooks, looking like white kites, were salted, dried fillets of cod fish: baccalà. Usually the market had another delicacy rarely seen today—tiny snails, blissfully sliding up and down wire mesh that covered basketfuls of them.

Nowadays, at my local market of Italian specialties, The Italian Store in Arlington, Virginia, the baccalà is kept in the back. Alex Locci, one of the chief honchos, will cut you a chunk. For some reason, this product does not smell the way it seemed to smell to me when I was a boy.

Regardless, here is one of the ways Mama made it for Papa, upon his fairly frequent requests, and one of the ways I now like it myself.

INGREDIENTS

1½ pounds dried baccalà

2 tablespoons fresh Italian parsley, chopped

1 tablespoon fresh dill or ½ teaspoon dried

¼ cup dry white wine

Extra virgin olive oil

4 lemons

Salt and freshly ground black pepper to taste

PREPARATION

Soak the baccalà under an inch or two of cold water, covered, in the refrigerator, for at least 48 hours, changing the water 3 times a day. This removes the salt and hydrates the fish.

With a sharp, pointed knife, carefully remove a thin film you're likely to find on one side of the fish, and any bones. Cut the baccalà into 3-inch squares.

For the poaching, place cold water in a 12-inch-wide pan up to a depth of a little more than inch. Add a tablespoon of the parsley and the dill, as well as the white wine and the juice of 1 of the lemons.

Boil the infused water for 10 minutes, and then put the baccalà in it. Bring the heat immediately to low and simmer for about 15 minutes or until the fish flakes.

Remove the baccalà from the water with a slotted spoon, pat it dry with paper towels, and let it cool for 2 minutes.

Drizzle olive oil over it and add salt and black pepper to taste, as well as rest of the chopped parsley and juice from the remaining 3 lemons.

Serves 4

Baccalà in Tomato Sauce with Onions, Olives, and Capers

Here's a version of the baccalà dish in *rosso,* or tomato sauce, instead of in *bianco,* herbs and wine. It's jazzed up a little from the way Mama made it.

INGREDIENTS

1½–2 pounds baccalà

2 tablespoons olive oil

2 large garlic cloves, chopped

Pinch of hot red-pepper flakes

32 ounces tomato purée, homemade or store-bought (imported)

Salt and ground black pepper to taste

½ white onion, thinly sliced

⅓ cup kalamata olives, washed

⅓ cup capers, washed

1½ tablespoons Italian parsley, chopped

PREPARATION

See the previous recipe for the soaking, cleaning, and cutting of the baccalà

Preheat the oven to 350 degrees. In a skillet over medium-high heat, sauté the garlic in 1 tablespoon of the olive oil. Add the hot pepper and tomato purée, and simmer until the sauce bubbles.

Gently rub salt and pepper onto both sides of the baccalà sections. Heat the remaining tablespoon of oil in a skillet, over medium-high heat. In it, sear the baccalà, about two minutes per side.

Place the baccalà in a baking dish and cover with the tomato sauce. Add the onion slices, kalamata olives, and capers, stirring so they are evenly distributed in the dish.

Bake in the oven for about 15 minutes or until the fish flakes. Sprinkle the baccalà with parsley and serve.

Serves 4

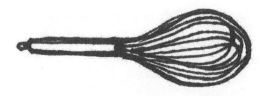

Zucchini alla Parmigiana:
A Twist on an Iconic Dish

Eggplant parmigiana is a must-have item on many Italian restaurant menus. Zucchini parmigiana is another matter. It's rarely seen on a menu. Eggplant reigns supreme.

Mama made eggplant parmigiana for decades. (Sister Alba says her husband, Jim Logan, of good Irish stock, insists he married her for Mama's eggplant parmigiana.) Later on, Mama switched to zucchini. She said it made the dish lighter. Both versions are favorites of mine, especially eaten in sandwiches a day or two after the original cooking.

Mama's offerings of these parmigianas were light and compact, by which I mean they were never watery—a bad circumstance among parmigianas I have ordered in restaurants. Her trick was in the preparation of the vegetables, whether eggplant or zucchini. They were dried before cooking, and they were sautéed in a little flour and beaten egg. No breadcrumbs. I repeat, no breadcrumbs, even though you will find that ingredient in most parmigiana recipes in existence. We were just not a breadcrumb family, I suppose, using it in very few recipes. (Two show up in this volume.) Hereabouts, standard breadcrumbs are considered, in most cases, to add unnecessary weight to perfectly good, plain food.

What follows is Mama's zucchini parmigiana recipe. Afterward, you'll find some words about eggplant parmigiana, especially Alba's version. It is world-class.

INGREDIENTS

1½ pounds zucchini

2 tablespoons extra virgin olive oil for the sauce

1 clove garlic

½ teaspoon salt

¼ teaspoon hot red-pepper flakes

2 cups homemade or purchased plain tomato purée

8-ounce can smooth tomato sauce, such as Del Monte's or Hunt's

1 tablespoon tomato paste (if necessary)

6 large basil leaves, roughly torn

Flour for dredging

1½ tablespoons olive oil and 1½ tablespoons vegetable oil, for frying

2 well-beaten eggs

2 cups freshly shredded mozzarella cheese

1 cup freshly grated Parmigiano Reggiano cheese

PREPARATION

Preheat the oven to 325 degrees. Wash the zucchini well and cut them crosswise in sections, 3 or 4 inches wide. With a sharp knife, slice the sections lengthwise in strips, about a quarter-inch thick, discarding the first slice containing mostly skin.

Lay the slices out flat on a broad dish or on paper towels and let them dry for about an hour. (You can add a light sprinkling of salt over the zucchini slices to make them "sweat.")

Meanwhile, start cooking the sauce. In a medium-sized saucepan, heat 2 tablespoons of the olive oil and add the garlic, either chopped or whole—the latter for eventual removal. Also add the pepper flakes. When the oil just begins to sizzle, add the tomato purée, the can of tomato sauce, and a little salt. Let the sauce simmer while preparing the zucchini, stirring occasionally. Add the basil.

After the zucchini have dried, dip the slices lightly in flour and lay them out again on a dish or paper towel. In a large skillet over medium-high heat, place the 3 tablespoons of oil, combining olive and another (nonheavy) vegetable oil in equal measures (a partnership for lightness sake).

Whisk the eggs in a large dish and dip in the floured zucchini slices until completely coated. Shake off any excess and return the slices to the dish. Drop a small piece of the zucchini into the oil. When it sizzles energetically, signifying the oil is hot enough, drop in the other slices. Lay them flat in the pan, not jumbled on top of one another.

Let the slices cook until they are light brown on both sides, about a minute per side. Remove them to paper towels to drain and continue cooking any remaining slices. Add more oil if necessary. Pat the slices dry with more paper towels.

Shred the mozzarella on the coarse-cut side of a grater, tearing up the "heel" that remains into small pieces. Grate the Parmigiano Reggiano, but more finely.

Spread tomato sauce lightly on the bottom of a high-sided glass baking dish. It can be square or round, with a cooking surface about 9 inches wide. Make sure the sauce has thickened and is not in any way watery. If it is, stir in some tomato paste and heat it again before proceeding. Lightly spread a layer of the grated Parmigiano over the tomato sauce. Then make a layer of the zucchini slices, having them touch on the sides as much as possible. Spread more Parmigiano over the zucchini, then a layer of the shredded mozzarella.

Then comes the tomato sauce, placed first around the inside edges of the dish and then over everything. Keep making layers until the slices are gone. On the top should be a layer of mozzarella, covered with sauce.

Cover the dish with foil and bake for about 25 minutes, or until you see the sauce and cheese bubbling slightly. Remove the dish from the oven and let it cool for a half-hour, preferably more. (For me, both zucchini and eggplant parmigianas are better lukewarm than hot, and can be sliced more easily the more they cool.)

Serves 4

Eggplant Parmigiana

The recipe for eggplant parmigiana is virtually the same as for the zucchini version. The difference is in the handling of the eggplant. Before anything is put together, the eggplant, peeled and sliced crossways, is laid out on paper towels, sprinkled with a little salt, and left to dry. The drying should be for several hours, and it can even be overnight. Then you're set to go, using the same steps as for the zucchini.

Alba's secret is to use a "mandolin" cutting device, available at many kitchen gadget stores, to make exceptionally thin slices of the eggplant. This enables her to make a cake-like parmigiana of many layers, as pleasing for its aesthetics as for its taste. The mandolin can also be used in making the zucchini parmigiana, but be prepared to spend more time cooking the slim slices.

SIDE DISHES

French-Toasted Grilled Cheese Sandwiches

In my elementary school days in old Newark, kids walked home for lunch. Mama, having taken time off from work to walk home for lunch herself, almost always had something hot waiting for me.

When there wasn't much time, she'd make something quickly, like these grilled cheese sandwiches. One of them would eliminate all hunger pangs until dinner. This is Mama's way of making them, with cheese alone. Feel free to add ham—turning the sandwich into a version of France's croque monsieur—and/or tomatoes.

This creation can serve as a "main" lunch course, as a snack any time of the day, or, cut into little crustless squares, as a hot appetizer or side serving next to soup.

INGREDIENTS

1 large egg

Salt and pepper to taste

Two slices of bread, either extra-thick white "American-style" bread, or crusty Italian bread, such as casareccia

2 slices of cheese, one cheddar and the other Swiss, neither slice being of the processed sort

1 tablespoon butter plus 1 tablespoon olive or vegetable oil

PREPARATION

Beat the egg well in a dish wide and steep enough to hold the sandwich. Add salt and freshly ground black pepper to the egg as you beat it.

Make a sandwich of the bread and cheese. Dip one side then the other in the egg, assuring that both sides are well-soaked.

In a nonstick pan over medium-high heat, bring the butter and oil to a bubble. Let any excess of the beaten egg drip from the sandwich. Place one side of the sandwich down in the butter and oil, and cook until browned. Turn the sandwich over and brown the other side. By now, the cheese should be oozing out of the bread.

At that point, it's done. Cool and eat.

Spicy Green Cauliflower

This is a great side dish—flavorful, nutritious, and somewhat mysterious-looking. It can be made with white or green cauliflower, the latter a cross between cauliflower and broccoli. With some of the green variety, the flowerets are pointed, so it's called *pyramid cauliflower*. I prefer the green cauliflower to the white; it's slightly sweeter, marginally more nutritious, and seems to remain firmer in cooking.

A key ingredient in this dish is hot red-pepper flakes; you can make the dish as hot as you like.

INGREDIENTS

1 large green head of cauliflower, washed, broken apart or cut into flowerets 1-inch to 1¼-inches around

2 tablespoons extra virgin olive oil, plus another tablespoon if needed

2 large garlic cloves, chopped

¼ teaspoon hot red-pepper flakes, or more if desired

Half of a lemon

¼ teaspoon coarse sea salt

PREPARATION

Steam the cauliflower flowerets in a large saucepan over a small amount of boiling water, until cooked through but still firm, 3 minutes or so. Remove them from the steamer pan, pat away excess moisture with paper towels, and set aside.

Heat two tablespoons of the oil in a broad sauté pan. Add the garlic and shake the pan as the garlic begins to get crispy. Add the hot pepper flakes.

Add the cauliflower flowerets and continue shaking as they warm, adding a small amount of oil if they look dry. Take care not to let the garlic burn, though some searing on the flowerets enhances their look and taste.

Squeeze the lemon all over the cauliflower and sprinkle on the sea salt. Stir vigorously and serve immediately.

Serves 4

The Amazing Round Zucchini: Recipe No. 1

I didn't know these vegetables existed until I saw them at a farmers' market: perfectly round zucchini. They have the shape and girth of a softball, and a little stub on top, just like the ordinary zucchini, which are shaped like elongated blackjacks.

These round zucchini taste like regular ones, but are fleshier. Because of their shape, they lend themselves nicely to the making of zucchini parmigiana, subject of an earlier recipe. The other use I like is as a grilled delicacy, described below.

Unfortunately, round zucchini are not easy to come by. Major grocery stores, in my area of northern Virginia at least, do not carry them. They can be found at farmer's markets, although the one in Falls Church that I frequent held just one stand that displayed round zucchini. You can grow your own, and a search of the web will yield several outfits willing to sell you seeds.

Here's my favorite thing to do with round zucchini, providing a simple, summery side-dish to just about anything:

Wash a large zucchini ball and place it on a cutting board, with the top stub and the bottom facing left and right. With a sharp knife, cut away the top and bottom, then make slices a quarter-inch thick, using the whole vegetable.

Put the slices on a paper towel and let them stand for a half-hour or more. Pat them dry, then sprinkle dried marjoram, a little sea salt, and pepper on both sides of each slice. Lightly brush both sides with olive oil.

Place the slices on a very hot charcoal or gas grill, turning them until dark burn marks appear on both sides. Continue cooking on a less hot part of the grill until the zucchini slices are soft and the green skins on them withered, about two to three minutes.

Remove the zucchini slices from the grill, salt them again if desired, and serve immediately. There will be enough slices from each zucchini "ball" to serve two or three people.

The Amazing Round Zucchini: Recipe No. 2

Here's another way to use these unusual vegetables. It's a variation of the zucchini parmigiana recipe shown earlier.

Preheat oven to 350 degrees. Prepare slices of the round zucchini as described on the previous page. Put on a hot grill just long enough for them to acquire slanted burn marks. For each of two servings, lightly oil a small baking dish.

Place one zucchini round at the bottom. On top of it, add a tablespoon of shredded mozzarella, then a thin slice of a ripe tomato. Place a second zucchini round on top of that, and add the mozzarella and tomato. Add a third zucchini round, topped with mozzarella and a sprinkling of Parmigiano Reggiano. On each layer, add a pinch of sea salt and freshly ground black pepper.

Bake until all the cheese has melted and the zucchini and tomato have softened, 10 to 15 minutes.

Little Zucchini Pizzas

These little treats can accompany anything, and they also can serve as a snack or an appetizer. They may turn a little mushy, depending on the freshness of the zucchini and the cooking time, but are tasty in any form.

INGREDIENTS

1 large yellow zucchini

1 large green zucchini

(Score the skins of both with a fork. Slice them lengthwise into ovals 2½–3 inches wide.)

Kosher salt and ground black pepper

Extra virgin olive oil

Small amount of panko for sprinkling

6–8 ounces fresh mozzarella

Basil leaves, equal in number to the zucchini slices

2 medium-sized plum tomatoes, sliced

PREPARATION

Preheat oven to 400 degrees. Sprinkle a little salt on the zucchini slices and let them "sweat" for about half an hour. Pat them dry and lightly sprinkle with salt and pepper. Put a few drops of oil on each slice. Arrange the slices on foil on a baking tray and bake until zucchini begins to soften slightly.

Remove the tray from the oven and then turn the oven to a high broil. Sprinkle the zucchini slices lightly with the panko and return them to the oven for about 2 minutes. Remove the slices again, and place a dollop of mozzarella, a basil leaf, and a slice of tomato—in that order—on each.

Place the slices in the oven again, just long enough for the cheese to turn soft. Serve with crusty Italian bread on the side.

Makes 4 side dishes

Yet Another Italian Soul Food: Giambotta

So many Italian dishes, especially from the South, have been given that soul-food label. This one comes closest to deserving it, in my opinion. It's a hearty vegetable stew that Mama made regularly. An excellent side dish at supper, it becomes a delicious all-in-one lunch reheated the next day. The preferred accompaniments are thick slices of toasted Italian bread.

INGREDIENTS

1 large eggplant, skinned and cut into 1-inch cubes

1 medium yellow zucchini, skin scored with a fork and cut into 1-inch cubes

1 medium green zucchini, skin scored with a fork and cut into 1-inch cubes

3 tablespoons extra virgin olive oil, plus more for drizzling

2 garlic cloves, minced

3 medium Yukon gold potatoes, peeled, cut into 1-inch cubes, and blanched for a couple minutes

½ cup carrots, cut into ¼-inch-wide rounds

1 cup green beans, cut into 1-inch pieces and blanched for a couple minutes

3 medium tomatoes, skinned, seeded, and cut into 1-inch pieces

1 small bunch fresh dandelion greens, roughly torn, excessively thick stems removed, and blanched for a couple minutes

1 large sweet red pepper, roasted, skinned, seeded, and cut into ½-inch wide slices lengthwise, then cut in half (The roasting and skinning can be avoided, but they do prevent the skin from twisting into sharp little spears.)

1 small white onion, thinly sliced, the rings then cut into 2-inch pieces

½ cup chicken stock

½ teaspoon marjoram

½ teaspoon thyme

Sea salt and freshly ground black pepper to taste

Freshly grated Parmigiano Reggiano (optional)

PREPARATION

Lay out the eggplant and zucchini cubes on paper towels and allow them to dry for an hour or more.

Heat the oil in an extra large skillet or stew pot. With the heat on high, quickly sauté the eggplant and zucchini until they have softened slightly. Add the garlic and lower the heat.

Add the potatoes, carrots, green beans, tomatoes, dandelions, pepper, onion, and chicken stock.

Add the marjoram, thyme, a sprinkling of sea salt, and generous and widely spread-out twists of the ground black pepper.

Stir well and cook, covered, over medium-low heat for 35 minutes, stirring occasionally. If there is too much liquid from the stock and vegetables, continue cooking uncovered for 15 more minutes. (Don't get rid of *all* the liquid. It's needed for bread-dunking later.)

Drizzle some olive oil on the giambotta and allow it to cool before serving. Some like a sprinkling of Parmigiano Reggiano on top.

Serves 4–6

More Giambotta—in a Pie

So here we were with a lot of leftover giambotta. My wife, Chris, found an imaginative use for it. She created a pie to put it in—a pie without the traditional thick crust. Her crust was phyllo. The result was a tasty side dish, like the pie's precursor, vegetable stew, or better yet, a lunch centerpiece.

INGREDIENTS

8 sheets phyllo, defrosted if previously frozen, ideally 9 by 14 inches

3 tablespoons melted butter and 3 tablespoons olive oil, mixed together

Bread crumbs

4 slices Swiss cheese

Grated Parmigiano Reggiano (pecorino may be substituted)

2 cups cooked giambotta, patted very dry with paper towels

Sea salt and freshly ground black pepper to taste

2 eggs plus 1 cup whole milk, beaten together

PREPARATION

Preheat oven to 375 degrees. Lay out a phyllo sheet on a flat surface and brush it with the butter and oil. Sprinkle it very lightly with bread crumbs. Repeat this with 3 more sheets. Then place the 4 sheets all together in a glass baking dish, 8 or 9 inches square by 2 inches high, or a 9-inch pie plate.

Repeat this with 4 more phyllo sheets and, when finished, lay them across the first set of layered sheets, so that one set of sheets faces north-south and the other east-west. The sheets will overlay the side of the backing dish. Snip off the excess phyllo, leaving enough to cover the "wall" of the dish. Crimp the phyllo tightly against the sides.

Cover the bottom of the crust with the Swiss cheese slices, and sprinkle some of the grated cheese lightly over the Swiss cheese.

Place the giambotta over the cheeses, pressing it down gently. Add some sea salt and black pepper to taste.

Pour the beaten eggs and milk over the giambotta, topped with a generous sprinkling of the grated cheese.

Bake the pie for about one hour, or until it is set, with a very brown, crusty, and bubbly top. Let the pie cool for at least a half-hour before serving.

Serves 6

Funghi Trifolati (A Sauté of Mushrooms)

Mushrooms are healthful, and here's an easy and tasty Italian-style way to make them. The varieties suggested for the dish are button or cremini, but others work as well.

INGREDIENTS

2 tablespoons olive oil

2 garlic cloves, whole

1 pound mushrooms, washed quickly, dried, and cut into ¼-inch slices lengthwise

Pinch of sea salt and freshly ground black pepper

½ tablespoon dry white wine

½ tablespoon fresh lemon juice

1 tablespoon chopped Italian parsley

PREPARATION

Heat the olive oil and garlic in a broad sauté pan over medium-high heat. Add the mushrooms, spreading them out as much as possible in the pan. When all the mushrooms are coated with oil, lower the heat to medium and cook, stirring, until mushrooms are cooked but still firm, about 5 or 6 minutes.

Add the salt and pepper, and the wine. Bring the heat to medium-high and continue cooking until most but not all the liquid has evaporated, about 4 minutes.

Discard the garlic cloves. Sprinkle the lemon juice over the mushrooms, stir in the parsley, and serve as a side dish.

Makes 4 side dishes

SWEETS

Intergenerational Raisin "Cookies"

These raisin cookies were an invention of Mama's and a great hit with the grandchildren. They were called cookies, though they were in the shape of small biscotti. The grown-ups liked them as much as the kids did. For the elders, they were not too sweet and were excellent accompaniments to espresso, an after-dinner cordial, or both. Here's the recipe, which exactly follows Mama's methods.

INGREDIENTS

1½ cups flour

3 teaspoons baking powder

¼ cup sugar

3 eggs

½ teaspoon cinnamon

Half-stick (4 ounces) unsalted butter

½ cup raisins (dried cranberries would do as well)

PREPARATION

Preheat oven to 325 degrees. Place the flour in a sifter, half a cup at a time. (Mama bragged about her sifter, which she said she had owned for 64 years, along with a huge metal colander that she owned for 60 years.) With each half-cup, add one teaspoon of the baking powder. When all is sifted, set aside.

Place the sugar and two of the eggs in a medium-sized bowl. Mix well with an electric egg beater. Add the cinnamon.

Cut the butter into chunks and melt them completely in a skillet. Add the melted butter to the sugar-and-egg mixture slowly, mixing well with a spoon or the egg beater.

Now comes a little physical exercise. Take about half a handful of the sifted flour and baking powder and add it, a bit at a time, to the sugar, egg, and butter mixture, stirring briskly with a wooden spoon until the flour is all absorbed. Repeat this—it will take at least a dozen repetitions—until almost all the flour has been stirred into the mixture. You'll know you're ready for the next step when you lift the spoon straight out and the mixture doesn't fall off.

Butter a 9-by-12-inch cookie sheet and sprinkle it with flour. Fold the raisins into the mixture. (You can use more than half a cup if you like raisins.)

Now flour your hands. This is important, because you're going to pick up the mixture, about two tablespoons at a time, and fashion it into cylinders about an inch and a half around and four to five inches long. If your hands are not floured, the mixture will stick stubbornly to your fingers. Mama didn't mold the mixture into shape so much as roll it into the cylinders on a flat surface. You should have enough of the mixture for four or five cylinders. Beat the yolk of the third egg and brush the tops of the cylinders lightly.

Bake for 25 minutes, checking at the 20-minute mark to make sure the bottoms are not burning. They should be medium-brown.

Let the cylinders cool for 10 minutes or so, then slice them at an angle, a half-inch or so wide. The cookies/biscotti—there should be 30 to 40 of them—are ready to be eaten.

Pizza Dolce: A Pie of Ricotta

This is the traditional Easter and Christmastime cheesecake of southern Italy. I waited eagerly for it every year as the holidays approached, because Mama made it superbly. Recipes for pizza dolce, or sweet pie, as the delicacy is called, vary only slightly. The chief elements that set Mama's version apart from most others I have seen is the presence of chocolate and the creaminess of the filling.

INGREDIENTS

For the crust:

2 cups all-purpose flour, sifted

¼ cup sugar

Pinch of salt

½ teaspoon grated lemon rind

4 ounces butter, cut in pieces

2 eggs, plus 2 beaten egg yolks (one of the yolks set aside)

For the filling:

1½ pounds whole milk ricotta

¼ cup heavy cream

⅓ cup sugar

2 eggs, plus 1 egg yolk

Grated rind of an orange

Grated rind of a lemon

1 teaspoon vanilla extract

1 tablespoon anisette

¼ cup citron pieces (Citron is hard to find in traditional, even upscale, markets, but it can be ordered from the Internet. Otherwise, dried, diced, and sugared pineapple or lemon work as substitutes.)

⅓ cup bittersweet chocolate broken into ½-inch-wide pieces

PREPARATION

Preheat oven to 350 degrees.

For the crust:

Mix the sifted flour, sugar, salt, and lemon zest together on a flat surface, and make a well in the middle. Gradually massage the butter pieces into the pile, then, a little at a time, the beaten eggs—the two whole eggs and one of the two yolks. Keep kneading the mixture until you have a smooth ball. Wrap it in plastic and refrigerate for 1 hour.

For the filling:

Beat together the ricotta, cream and sugar. Gradually add the eggs, mixing everything together very well. While continuing to mix thoroughly, add the orange and lemon gratings, the vanilla extract, the anisette, the citron, and the chocolate.

Remove the dough for the crust from the refrigerator and slice away about a third of it to be used later for the top of the pizza dolce. Roll the larger piece flat, adding flour if it is too moist. It may be easier for you to flatten it by hand. The circumference should be sufficient to cover the bottom and sides of a buttered 9-inch pie plate.

Pour the filling evenly into the crust. Roll out the remainder of the dough and cut it with a sharp knife into eight to ten strips about three-quarters of an inch wide. Place the strips on top of the filling, and then beat the remaining egg yolk to use as a "wash" over the strips on top as well as on the exposed sides of the crust.

Bake the pizza dolce for about 45 minutes, or more, until the crust turns light brown and a toothpick in the center comes out clean.

Let the pie sit before serving, until lukewarm—or even better, cool. Favored accompaniments: hot espresso coffee and, yes, a shot of anisette.

Makes up to 8 servings

Eat It Straight from the Icebox

That's what we did, more so than eating it at the table as a dessert, although that was fine too. We're talking about a light and airy, but wholesome, "icebox cake," requiring no baking. It's a layered creation consisting of chocolate pudding, graham crackers, and banana. For Mama, it was cheap and quick to make, and, day or night, the perfect snack.

Mama almost always had a tray of this sweet in the fridge, alternating with Jell-O. Anyone seeing me march toward the fridge with spoon in hand would know I was going after one or the other. Open the fridge, take one or two quick, cool spoonfuls—a delightful, curiously restorative mouthful—and close the fridge.

Lest you worry about the effect of chocolate pudding on the waistline, pudding, nowadays, unlike in the early days, is available with no fat or sugar, and the milk with which it's made can be skim.

INGREDIENTS

1 package chocolate pudding mix, preferably fat- and sugar-free, yielding two cups of pudding

2 cups skim milk

7 or 8 graham crackers

1 large banana

PREPARATION

Following package directions, cook the pudding in the milk until it has thickened. Place graham crackers on the bottom of a 9-by-5-inch loaf pan. After the pudding has cooled slightly, spread a thick layer of it over the crackers.

Slice the banana into rounds and place half of the pieces over the pudding. Then comes a layer of crackers, followed by the pudding, followed by the rest of the banana.

Finally, lay down crackers over the bananas and the rest of the pudding over the crackers, smoothing it with a spatula.

Cover the "cake" lightly with wax paper and cool several hours in the fridge. Then grab a spoon.

If passing out at the table, this recipe makes 4–5 servings

Part III:
The "Holy Grail"

Pullia

This is about one of the most unusual and little-known dishes in the glorious universe of Italian cooking. When Mama made it, the family converged on her kitchen as bees to honey; in fact, the sly woman sometimes used it as a lure to get us to visit. And yet I hesitated before deciding to include it in this volume, for two reasons.

One reason is that its main ingredient—what our family calls pullia (poo-LEE-ah), an obscure member of the mint family—is not easily obtained. It's not sold in any food store in America that I know of, although I have found it in herb nurseries here and there. Even in Italy, it is apparently a regular ingredient in only a few small towns in the south, one of which where my mother and father were born. People within a few miles of these towns have never heard of it. In those communities, including Mirabella Eclano (my parents' hometown), Grottaminarda, and Bonito, as in the kitchens of my extended family in America, it is cooked into simple tomato sauce and served, preferably, with tiny homemade cavatelli, sometimes called cicatelli.

The other reason I hesitated to write about pullia is that, under certain circumstances and in certain quantities, it can be poisonous—known to induce miscarriages, damage livers, even kill. For centuries, one of the things it has been to known to kill is fleas. This final attribute is how pullia (one of the ways it is known in the vernacular) got its more high-sounding scientific designation, *Mentha pulegium*. The "pul" comes from the Latin *pulex*, which means "flea." In Roman times, the scholar Pliny sang the praises of *Mentha pulegium* as an efficient terminator of fleas, for whom the Eternal City was—and remains—a happy hunting ground.

In some towns, the herb is spelled pulieio and pronounced poo-LAY-oh. It is also known in some parts of southern Italy as puleggio. The modern English name is more recognizable: pennyroyal.

So this is what I had to consider: did I want to tout a dish made with a certain herb that is not easily available and can be poisonous, most notably to fleas but also to humans? The near-fanatical regard in which pullia is held by the relatively few people on this earth who know and use it in the way I describe argued yes. There is something about pasta-and-pullia that is habit-forming. Not in the sense that one has to have it all the time, like a drug, but in the sense that, upon finishing a plate, one looks immediately forward to the next serving, whether that be a week, month, or year hence.

Pullia is among hundreds of herbs in the mint family, but its taste and aroma are unique. Both taste and smell are robust without being overpowering. I think the word that best describes its effect on the eater is *heady*. It's as if pullia were the wise old patriarch of all mints, distilling the essence of the entire family, its gravitas contrasting with the more mundane family members like peppermint and spearmint.

Some in my family at one point thought catnip, that other mint that is the object of olfactory lust, was really pullia. Just as there are some cats that turn their noses up at catnip, there are some people who are not taken by pullia. The Rodale Herb Book (1974), for instance, calls pennyroyal "a totally insignificant plant." But the naysayers are few and certainly include no one in my extended family. Nor are there many who dislike pullia, I am sure, among the citizens of Mirabella Eclano, Grottaminarda, and Bonito.

Far from those towns where pullia is easy to find on the ground (where it grows wild in watery surroundings) or in farmers' markets, relatives of mine here in America have contented themselves with small amounts, cooked or traded in modest quantities. The main source of pullia for most of my immediate family, aside from a batch that my wife, Chris, and I brought to the United States from Italy, is my cousin Rosanella. She and her husband, Sam, have succeeded in growing it in reasonable quantities in their backyard in New Jersey.

It was only recently that I discovered that some plant and herb nurseries, at least in the East, have been carrying pennyroyal. Packaged as tiny plants in cardboard or plastic boxes, it is generally described as an ingredient for potpourri or tea, although when I asked one purveyor in New Jersey to describe its use, he said, "I have no idea." One wholesaler, from Australia, incongruously describes the perennial pennyroyal on its herb tag this way: "Insect repellent for fleas, ants, and mosquitoes. Sparingly used with potatoes and to flavour cream cheese."

An Herb of the Old Country—and the New

I long thought Rosanella and Sam were growing pullia from seeds sent to them from Italy. But it turned out that their pullia was not the original European version that enriches supper tables in Mirabella Eclano and nearby towns. Found growing wild in their yard, it is "American" pullia, officially designated *Hedeoma pulegioides*. It has flowers slightly different from the European variety's frizzy purple buds, but the small leaves are virtually the same. Moreover, according to an expert I consulted, Dr. James Duke, a famous botanist based in Maryland, the American and European pullia mints are so close to being identical that they are nearly interchangeable, having virtually the same composition. It takes a very sensitive nose and palate to tell the difference. The pennyroyal I found at a couple of nurseries near me in Virginia was of the European strain, from long-ago transplanted roots.

So this is one of my justifications for telling you about pullia. It may take years, if ever, before the delicate, stringy, leafy stalks of pullia are sold in American supermarkets along with the more familiar greens and herbs. But I was surprised to find local nurseries selling the European pullia, under its English name, pennyroyal. And the American variation also grows among us, mostly, it seems, in the eastern part of the country, though the herb is reported to have been found in the West as well. It takes a practiced eye to spot it among weeds in low, wet areas. But it can be found, and, if carefully picked, with tiny roots intact, can be replanted in anybody's backyard.

The recognition of the sparse but real availability of pullia in America left the other reason for my hesitation in writing about it: the potential for the meek-looking herb to be poisonous. Not that I believe the pullia dish, as prepared by our family and thousands of people in the few "pullia towns" in Italy, has ever made or could ever make anyone sick. Indeed, from antiquity, the herb was not only used as a savory ingredient in cooking, but as a medicine.

Ancient Herbs, a book by Marina Heilmeyer, published in 2007 by the J. Paul Getty Museum, cited Pliny's suggestion that the grated seeds of pennyroyal could purify contaminated water. The Roman sage, Ms. Heilmeyer, writes, "recommended sniffing finely chopped pennyroyal mixed with some vinegar as a cure for fainting spells. Dried and finely grated, the herb could allegedly fortify the gums; puréed with barley groats, it made a compress to cure all kinds of inflammation; boiled down and used as a bath salt, it relieved itchings; and cooked and mixed with vinegar water, it cured nausea, vomiting, and stomachache." In addition, according to the website herb-magic.com, pennyroyal can also ward off the evil eye if mixed with nettle and graveyard dirt and sprinkled on hair and clothing.

Heilmeyer also refers to a Roman-era cookbook by Apicius containing a recipe for a purée of squash, flavored with pennyroyal, that "was apparently such a popular dish that it was still being prepared centuries later in the kitchens of medieval cloisters." Heilmeyer says pennyroyal's use in medicine and cooking extended into the seventeenth century when "it retreated into obscurity, pushed aside by peppermint ... which arose by chance in England."

The obscurity wasn't total, of course. At least not in the above mentioned towns in southern Italy. Nor among those people who, to this day, enjoy pennyroyal tea. That includes the same Dr. Duke, who every so often drops a few leaves in hot water, claiming the drink "clears the head." The tea is also believed to settle the stomach, which is the use, some believe, the late

Kurt Cobain alluded to when his grunge band Nirvana recorded the song "Pennyroyal Tea" in 1993.

Still, there is no question that in a certain form, pennyroyal is dangerous. That form is its essential oil, achieved through a chemical process called distillation. Although it has a benign use as aromatherapy, the oil, if taken internally, can damage the liver and cause abortions. At least one woman is known to have died from drinking a small amount of the oil. It's believed an ounce of pure essential oil can kill, if taken internally.

But, as Dr. Duke related to me, it's all a matter of form and quantity. Pennyroyal consumption, in my definition, consists of absolutely no distilled essential oil. Rather, it deals only with leaves—either dried, as my relatives in America use them, or frozen and defrosted, as the cooks in the Italian towns use them.

Leaves, Yes; Essential Oil, No

As to the way Dr. Duke uses the leaves—in tea—he says, "It would take 400 cups of pennyroyal tea [at once] to kill me. Like other herbal drinks, it's less toxic than coffee." He uses a few leaves for every cup of tea. None of the dangerous distilled essential oil goes into the beverage. To distill pennyroyal into an ounce of essential oil, he and other experts I have consulted say you'd need well upward of a pound of pennyroyal leaves.

The standard recipe (below), which is made with pasta for four to six people, calls for only about half a cup of loosely packed dried leaves, weighing barely an ounce, to be included in an ample quantity of tomato sauce. In addition, Dr. Duke points out that some of the essential oil dissipates with the drying of the leaves, and also dissipates in the cooking.

A quotation from the book *Medicinal Spices,* by Eberhard Teuscher and two others, published in Germany in 2006, nicely sums up both sides of the issue: "Based on the existing data, there is no acute or chronic toxicity with the normal use of European pennyroyal as a seasoning." The book adds this: "The *essential oil* [my emphasis] from European pennyroyal is hepatotoxic [toxic to the liver] due to its pulegone [a compound derived from the essential oil of certain mint plants] content."

In other words, go ahead and season (as in the pullia dish), but avoid the oil. (The book does not recommend using European pennyroyal in tea.) Still, some advise against pregnant women partaking of pennyroyal even in nondistilled form, the concern being that if there were a miscarriage, it would be possible to wrongly blame it on the herb.

Just about everyone I know who is familiar with this unique pasta dish is totally oblivious to the herb's dark side (the essential-oil side) because, to their knowledge, and to the knowledge of everyone *they* know, no one has ever gotten sick from eating nondistilled pullia and cicatelli. That's the case at Ariano Irpino Hospital, the centrally located hospital for Mirabella Eclano and the nearby pullia towns. Asked if he knew of anyone from the area who had ever been sickened from eating pullia, the hospital director, Dr. Otto Ottosavino, unhesitatingly declared: "Absolutely not." Even the US Food and Drug Administration sanctions the use of pennyroyal as a flavoring in food in an appropriate amount (Code of Federal Regulations Title 21, Part 172).

I felt a need to trace pullia-with-pasta to its ancestral source, where my mother and father first tasted it as children, and where thousands of people in just a few localities (to my knowledge) cook it regularly today. That meant a trip to Italy, in search of the "holy grail."

So in late spring 2009, my wife, Chris, and I set out for the town where my parents were born, Mirabella Eclano, a community of slightly more than eight thousand souls stretched out on a low ridge of the rolling green Appennine Mountains, about forty miles northeast of Naples. Reached by a leisurely and panoramic three-hour drive from Rome, Mirabella Eclano is skirted by the famous Via Appia (Appian Way), the ancient stone road leading from Rome to the southernmost points of the Italian peninsula. This is the same road on which, an apocryphal version of the Bible states, St. Peter encountered the risen Jesus and asked, *"Quo vadis?"* or "Where are you going?" Jesus responded that he was heading toward Rome to be crucified again, whereupon Peter, who had been heading out of the capital, got the nerve to return and eventually face his upside-down crucifixion. (*Quo Vadis*, the movie, came out in 1951, starring Robert Taylor and Deborah Kerr.)

Mirabella Eclano gets half its name from Aeclanum, a town first settled in the third century BC. Its gray-brick, truncated ruins still stand right on the Via Appia, a bit northeast of the center of Mirabella. It originally was home to the Samnite tribe, which eventually was conquered by the Romans.

Aside from its Roman history, and aside from pullia, Mirabella Eclano's other claim to fame is a spectacular annual ceremony that draws thousands, including pilgrims from abroad. It's the procession of *Il Carro*, meaning "the wagon" or "the cart." This is a wagon or cart like no other. It is an eighty-foot-high tower of wood and hand-worked straw resembling the narrow front of a cathedral, with a statue of the Virgin Mary at its pinnacle.

This is the town's feast day of the *Madonna Addolorata* (Sorrowful Virgin Mary), held on the Saturday before the third Sunday in September. As closely packed worshippers press forward on a narrow street, they are followed by the teetering *carro*, which is pulled slowly by six long-horned oxen. A video of this unusual event on YouTube (search "Il carro of Mirabella Eclano") brings to mind a slow-motion, nonviolent running of the bulls at Pamplona.

As the oxen strain to pull, the huge Virgin Mary-topped icon is held erect by many men straining upon ropes attached to it. Some in the vicinity pray that the *carro* stays erect, because, in addition to possibly beaning people, its collapse is believed to foretell bad luck. The town's website recounts that the tower fell in 1881 and 1961, and that the region suffered a famine in 1882 and an earthquake in 1962. It's not known what unfortunate events triggered all the other famines and earthquakes that have befallen the area through the ages.

An Earthquake, a Slightly Changed Town

In fact, without a known harbinger of bad luck, a 6.8-magnitude earthquake struck on November 23, 1980, killing 4,575 people in the region, injuring 7,750, and leaving 250,000 homeless. I remember my mother waiting anxiously for word of relatives in the days following the disaster. None of her or my father's blood relatives were hurt, but Aunt Electra, the wife of my father's brother Sabato, lost several cousins. They reportedly were playing cards in a club when the roof fell in and crushed them.

That 1980 earthquake is the reason why, on this visit with Chris, Mirabella Eclano did not look exactly as it had to me during my first and only previous visit in the midsixties. Then, it had had a more rustic and lived-in feel.

This time, there were still some cobblestone streets, along with the simple white stucco church of St. Francis and the civic square, containing the intricately carved miniobelisk resembling the design of the September *carro*. From the square, looking out beyond giant fir trees, the eye sweeps over a bright green landscape far below, dotted with neat geometric shapes of worked land. But many of the buildings, rebuilt after the quake, had a more modern, Spartan look. In fact, work was underway on something once so out-of-place in an old Italian hilltop town—a huge concrete parking garage.

I had called ahead to two first cousins—Giuseppina, a spinster shopkeeper in her eighties who was the last Mazzarella living in Mirabella Eclano, and her brother Emiliano, retired head of the Naples-area division of Italy's social security system. He had said he and his wife, Anna, a retired schoolteacher, would travel from Naples to Mirabella Eclano to meet us.

As we pulled up to the Mazzarella shop on Via Roma, easy to spot with foot-high letters of the name above the doorway, Giuseppina came out to meet us. I hadn't seen her in more than forty years. She was as imposing a woman as I remembered; the years hadn't dimmed the sparkle in her eyes or the easy smile. Dark-haired and rosy-cheeked, dressed in a multicolored silk blouse and black skirt, she seemed to enjoy more vitality than the typical octogenarian.

This was the same Giuseppina who had written her Uncle Pasquale, my father, in 1953, thanking him for sending packages to her family in Mirabella Eclano (see Pasquale's Story). The parcels had contained goods, she said, that had helped her to avoid being left behind fashion-wise, and thus making a *"brutta figura,"* [bad impression] in a town where poor young girls were trying to look good in clothes and slathering on makeup.

Giuseppina had been in her early twenties when she'd written that letter. Now, here she was, more than half a century later, much better off, with lipstick and rouge carefully applied, dressed smartly, the grande dame of Via Roma.

The store she operates had been in the family for a very long time. Wording under the sign with the family name proclaimed its featured items as "Paper, Books, Profumes, Toys." But inside, in addition to these products, you could also buy anything from toothpaste to handbags. These days, it doesn't do all that much business, Emiliano later told me, but it is Giuseppina's life and she intends to run it until she dies.

Unfortunately, the sundries shop that Mama's family ran didn't survive the years. We went looking for it. Emiliano pointed out the site. It was a shuttered garage at No. 8 Via Eclano.

The Mazzarella store and the large living quarters attached to it had been badly damaged in the 1980 earthquake. Giuseppina had escaped unscathed. The structure was rebuilt with the help of government funding. Unlike some other buildings, though, it looked little different from how I remembered it: tall, wide windows in the front, with a stuccoed apartment above. The back of the store led to Giuseppina's dining room, with various pictures of saintly icons looking down from the walls, and then to the kitchen. The back porch off the kitchen afforded a vast panorama of the valley. On my previous visit, when there had been many more people living in the house, I had seen gleaming white globes of fresh cheeses hanging from the porch rafters.

I had sent word to Giuseppina that one of the reasons for our visit, in addition to renewing acquaintances with very *simpatico* and close relatives, was to investigate the source of pullia. There was a possibility, I feared, that the prized herb itself had become a distant memory in Mirabella Eclano. Perhaps no one grew it or used it anymore.

But when we arrived and asked about pullia, she replied quickly, "I'm having some delivered this afternoon." And so, a little later, the pullia arrived, brought by a lady from the farmers' market, along with vegetables Giuseppina had ordered. Giuseppina ripped open the plastic bag and out tumbled handfuls of the bright green pullia leaves, their stems attached.

The leaves and stems seemed more robust than both the American pullia growing wild in Rosanella's and Sam's yard and the European sprig that Dr. Duke had given me from his Maryland estate. Maybe it was only natural that pullia should be more robust in the land of its discovery and original fame.

Freezing the "Holy Grail"

Whatever the differences, for us, this was a "Holy Grail" moment. It was the most pullia I had ever seen in my life, and it was fresh, not dried, as we were accustomed to seeing back home. With pullia being so accessible in Italy, there is no need to dry it. The locals just wash it and freeze it in plastic bags, until the leaves are needed for sauce. Giuseppina showed us some of the bags in her freezer, each containing enough pullia for one supper. The next day, as we were visiting other, more distant relatives (Rosanella's brother's family), the lady of the house opened her freezer and showed us *her* stacked bags of identically frozen pullia. With a touch of sadness, I thought of my relatives in America—my brother and sister, their children, and various cousins—and how they had to be content with frugal donations of the virtually identical but still scarce American pullia from Rosanella and Sam. That situation should change, I thought, now that scattered nurseries have been found to carry pennyroyal plants.

In Mirabella Eclano that fine spring day, I got to sample pullia at its source, the place where it was a culinary favorite going back to Roman times. Giuseppina served it to Chris and me, and to cousin Emiliano and his wife, Anna, just as Mama had made it, steeped in simple, smooth tomato sauce. The only difference was that Giuseppina hadn't had time to make the customary accompaniment to this sauce—tiny, homemade gnocchi-like pasta called cicatelli. On this day, she used commercially made cavatelli instead.

The dish was amazing, redolent of the herb's dusky mint flavor and aroma, mingled with the tomato and pasta. The taste of Giuseppina's pullia seemed more subtle than the version we were accustomed to in America, owing possibly to its being used frozen instead of dried. At the table, we marveled at the uniqueness of the pullia and the fact that it was so little known, even in Italy. Emiliano said that none of his acquaintances in Naples, only forty miles away from where we sat, had ever heard of it.

The near anonymity of pullia was confirmed for us the next day when we visited an adjacent town where pullia is known and used. This was Grottaminarda, just northeast of Mirabella Eclano. Both towns have about the same population, slightly more than eight thousand. At a farmers' market in the fountain-dominated central piazza of Grottaminarda, Chris and I found not one but two women selling pullia. (The cost: one Euro, which is about one dollar and thirty cents, for a one-pound bag.) A shopper came up as we talked to one of the pullia sellers and wanted to know what "that herb" was. She said she had never seen it, smelled it, or heard of it, and she lived barely a twenty-minute drive away, in Benevento, a provincial capital.

Yet, in one closer place, the herb is a central star in a community feast. That place is the town of Bonito, population twenty-five hundred, six miles north of Mirabella Eclano. In most years, on a day in August, townspeople come together for the "Sagra (Festival) of Cecatiello (the above-mentioned cicatelli) and Pulieio." The feast-day dish is served virtually as my mother and relatives of Mirabella Eclano serve their version, the only difference being that the Bonito residents crush the "pulieio" with mortar and pestle instead of using the leaves whole.

Farther south, in the adjacent region of Basilicata, the herb has attained pseudo-sacred status, in the form of an ancient, ruined chapel the locals call Madonna del Puleggio. Maurizio Crocco, whose olive-growing family owns the surrounding land, said the ruins are centuries-old. His grandmother told him of the pullia's/pulleggio's Madonna role. Although the herb is plentiful in the area—plentiful enough to be associated in folklore with Mary, the mother of Christ—Signor Crocco was ignorant of any culinary use of it. "It's all over the place," he said. "I smell it. But that's it." He did not find it unusual for puleggio to have a Madonna association. After all, there are, for instance, Madonnas of oaks, olives, and orange trees, as well. Whether anyone has ever actually uttered a prayer to pennyroyal isn't known.

So now that we had found pullia, in all its ancestral abundance, the next question was, how did we get it home to Virginia? Between what Giuseppina had given us and what we had bought at the Grottaminarda farmers' market, we had a large quantity, perhaps two pounds. In addition, overhearing us talking about pullia to the clerk, a local diner at the hotel, a doctor, brought us a small cache of *his* pullia, adding to our hoard. We couldn't bring all of that back home without drying it. Where to do that? We found the answer in our small hotel on the main highway outside of town. In the back of the hotel, away from most guest traffic, there were broad landings between the floors. These landings had large windows that let in a lot of sun. There, we spread out our pullia, on cardboard, to dry. There were no complaints from hotel staff or other guests.

Onto the Plane with the "Pullia House"

After a day, the pullia was dry enough to be packed for travel. We also had two "live" stalks, with leaves and wispy roots. Chris took over their care and feeding. She slid the roots into water-filled plastic sleeves used to keep roses fresh. Then she taped the stalks inside a large aluminum bowl we bought locally. That's how they traveled to America—in carry-on baggage, inside what we referred to as "the pullia house." We planted these Italian imports near our home in Virginia; they didn't last very long in the foreign soil and climate. (The European pennyroyal acquired from Dr. Duke in Maryland is flourishing as of this writing, as are some little pots of the herb from local nurseries.) Still, we were satisfied, having successfully sought out the "holy grail" in its original habitat.

And now the bottom line: how do you nurture and dine with this strange herb? First, you have to acquire it. The American pennyroyal may be found growing anywhere but, as mentioned earlier, is difficult to identify. As to the European pennyroyal, three or four little pots can be bought at nurseries. They can be set out to grow together in a very large planter or in the ground, far from other vegetation. They thrive in places that get both sun and shade, and need plenty of water. The vine-like stalks grow flat, that is, horizontally, if they are of the European strain, or upright if they are of the American variety. There is an abundance of small leaves.

Snip the desired quantity of stalks and leaves, rinse them lightly, and use a paper towel to tap out most of the moisture. The leaves can be air-dried completely and put in jars. For a quicker way of drying, the stalks can be laid flat between two paper towels and microwaved for about two minutes. The dried leaves can then be easily pulled from the stalks, which are discarded. (We found this process, referring to all herbs, described in *Cook's Illustrated* magazine.) Set the leaves aside.

For the pasta, see the recipe for "Fresh Cavatelli and Broccoli Rabe." The pasta is a simple combination of flour and water. The "cicatelli" that the aficionados refer to for this dish are just tinier cavatelli, achieved by cutting the dough into tiny squares and rolling the little pieces off the thumb. Mama did that expertly, with both thumbs going at once. No one in the family has mastered this trick. A similar result can be obtained by rolling the dough into tiny balls and then pressing in one side of them with the point of a finger or the edge of a spoon handle. Some shops selling Italian specialties carry imported pasta in smaller shapes, labeled "cavatellini." They are no bigger than half an inch long and very close to Mama's version. They work well, as do the slightly bigger cavatelli. Whether homemade or store-bought, there ought to be about a pound of pasta for this dish.

For the sauce, start off with a large clove of garlic and a quarter teaspoon of hot red pepper flakes sautéed in hot olive oil until the oil sizzles slightly. Add a loosely packed, quarter of a cup of dried pullia, and sauté for a minute or two. Add about thirty ounces of strained, unflavored tomatoes, either homemade or store-bought, and a little salt. (The sauce should be smooth. Chopped or diced tomatoes compete with both the pullia and the pasta, and don't go with this dish. Neither does grated cheese, for most people.) Stir in a second quarter of a cup of pullia, and bring the sauce to a low boil. (Store leftover pullia in a glass jar in a dark, cool place.) Reduce the heat and simmer for a half-hour or more. Discard the garlic clove. In the meantime, boil the pasta in lightly salted water. When it is *al dente*, drain the pasta and mix it thoroughly with the sauce. Add a tablespoon of the cooking water to the sauce if it looks too thick.

As a main course, this serves four people; as a first course, six. Consider the diners inductees into the centuries-old fraternity of pullia devotees.

The dish was a favorite of Mama's in *her* century of living—part of her legacy to her survivors, along with other kitchen creations. The recipes take their places alongside other memories of a deceptively simple Italian immigrant woman—almost a supercentenarian—with a personality and character as intriguing as this, her signature dish.

Acknowledgments

This book is about family. Members of mine had a big hand in it. My brother Bud and sister Alba were their usual good-natured selves as we compared memories of my mother, father, and other relatives. Both read the manuscript at various times, correcting a fact here, laughing at the recollection of a family foible there. Their help was invaluable.

Our cousin Rosanella Ferrara, who lived around the corner from my mother and was in her house often, provided important information about how Mama produced certain dishes when we siblings were not around. Rosanella and her husband, Sam, for years were the sole keepers of homegrown pullia, the "holy grail" herb, and generously made it available to others in the family.

Farther afield, my cousins in Italy, Giuseppina and her brother Emiliano Mazzarella, not only offered hospitality when my wife, Chris, and I visited, but also gladly recounted family lore and, most important, told us of the care and use of pullia in their environs.

Pullia was the name we in the family gave to the obscure herb. Dr. Jim Duke, the famous and erudite botanist, called it by its proper English name, pennyroyal. He had me at his home and beautiful grounds in Maryland twice to help me understand the properties of the weed-like perennial.

My thanks to my daughters, Laura, Julie, and Lilianna, in their capacity as tasters of and commenters upon new dishes Chris and I dreamed up at our house.

Finally, there was a reader who inspired and prodded and edited me continually. She kept coming up with key fixes and suggestions. That person was Chris. Her contributions to the book are great. Nevertheless, responsibility for any remaining mistakes, illiteracies, or culinary heresies is mine alone.

Credits

Cover Photo and other photos: Various family sources.
Graphic Illustrations: Stephanie Goodrich
"Grandma Cooks" Video: Kitty Mazzarella
Cover Design: Luiza Kleina
Book Design: Steven Matlock
Author Photo: Paul Fetters

Index

Page numbers with *italic "ph"* indicate a photo on the page

Made in the USA
Lexington, KY
07 September 2012